JESUS for LITTLE ONES

JESUS *for* LITTLE ONES

Illustrated Bible Stories for Children

Illustrated by Helen Caswell

Text adapted from the original by Charles Foster

BROADMAN
&HOLMAN
PUBLISHERS

Nashville, Tennessee

4240-11
0-8054-4011-9

Dewey Decimal Classification: J220.95
Subject Heading: Bible Stories \ Jesus Christ
Library of Congress Card Catalog Number: 94-8886

Library of Congress Cataloging-in-Publication Data
Jesus for little ones : illustrated Bible stories for children / illustrated by Helen Caswell; text adapted from the original by Charles Foster.
    p. cm.
  Based on: First steps for little feet in Gospel paths / Charles Foster.
  ISBN 0-8054-4011-9
  1. Jesus Christ—Biography—Juvenile literature. 2. Bible stories, English—N.T. Gospels. [1. Jesus Christ—Biography. 2. Bible stories—N.T.] I. Caswell, Helen Rayburn, ill. II. Foster, Charles, 1822-1887. First steps for little feet in Gospel paths.
BT302.J55   1994
232.9'01—dc20   94-8886
[B]   CIP

Contents

Preface for Parents

Jesus for Little Ones was originally written in 1882 by Charles Foster as *First Steps for Little Feet in Gospel Paths*. Foster first told these Bible stories about Jesus to children in kindergarten classes before collecting them all in print. Much of Foster's original work has been preserved, along with the questions he asked the children after telling them a story. With Helen Caswell's new illustrations, the old, old story is given a fresh look for telling over and over again.

Jesus for Little Ones will virtually walk your child through Jesus' life, with all His teachings and miracles. And it will explain to your child in simple language the reason Jesus came to earth to be our Savior. You may wish to read the stories to your child, or give the book to your children who are already reading. The questions following each story about Jesus will help explain the story and reinforce its message. You may wish to adapt them to the individual age and personality of each child. Each story with its questions can be used for a daily devotional time with your child. The appropriate Bible references for each story are placed at the bottom of the page, should you or your child choose to follow up the story by reading the Bible account.

1. Jesus Is Born

The angels live up in heaven with God. God's Son lives there, too. His name is Jesus. A long time ago, God sent His Son Jesus to live in this world where we live. Here is how it happened.

In a country very far away from here there was a city. A city is a place where there are a lot of houses and people. This city was called Bethlehem. It was in a country far across the ocean.

One day a young woman named Mary went to Bethlehem. Her husband was named Joseph. Mary and Joseph did not live in Bethlehem; it was not their home. They went there to visit only for a short time. So they went to a house called an inn. An inn is a place where people who are visiting from another city can go to sleep.

But this inn was full of people. The man at the inn said there was no room for Mary and Joseph to sleep. So Mary and Joseph went to the stable to sleep.

A stable is a place where horses and cows sleep. There is a place in the stable for horses to lie down, and there is a place for them to eat. The place where they eat is called a manger.

You eat out of a plate or a bowl, but horses eat out of a manger. When a person feeds his horse, he pours some corn into the manger. Then the horse puts its mouth down into the manger and eats the corn. There was a manger in the stable where Mary and Joseph went to spend the night.

It was dark. It was not the right time to put corn in the manger for the horse to eat. But the manger was not empty. No, if you had been there and looked into it, you would have seen a little baby in the manger.

This baby was named Jesus, and Jesus was God's Son. God sent Jesus to Mary so He could live in the world with us. Since Mary did not have a nice cradle in the stable in which to lay her baby in there in the stable. So when she had wrapped some clothes around Him, she laid him in the manger His cradle.

1. God's Son lives in heaven. What is His name?
2. Did Jesus come to the world where we live?
2. What was His mother's name?
3. Why didn't Mary and Joseph stay at the inn?
4. Where did they go to sleep?
5. What do horses eat from in a stable?
6. What was this baby's name?

You can find this story in your Bible in Matthew 1:18-25 and Luke 2:1-7.

2. Shepherds Go to the Stable

In the countryside near Bethlehem the people used to have a lot of sheep to take care of. These sheep stayed out in the fields to eat the grass. But sometimes wild animals like bears and wolves came into the fields and hurt the sheep. So some men had to stay with the sheep to take care of them and keep the wild animals away.

The men who stayed to take care of the sheep were called shepherds. They stayed with the sheep in both the day, and in the night, too, because the night was when the wild animals came to try to hurt the sheep.

On the same night that baby Jesus was born in the stable some shepherds were in the field nearby. They were taking care of their sheep. All of a sudden an angel came down from heaven and spoke to them.

When the shepherds saw the angel they were afraid, because they had probably never seen an angel before.

But the angel told them not to be afraid because he had come to tell them good news. A little baby had been born, he said, to be their Savior. The angel was talking about Jesus, and he called Jesus the Savior.

Why did the angel call Jesus the Savior? Suppose something scary was about to happen to you, but suddenly someone came and rescued you. That person would have *saved* you. Jesus came to save us from our sins, which are the bad things we do. He came to save us from being punished for our sins after we die. That is why we call Him our Savior.

After the angel told the shepherds that Jesus was born he said they could see Jesus if they would go to Bethlehem. They would find Jesus in a stable lying in a manger.

Then the shepherds said to each other, "Let us go and see this little baby that God sent his angel to tell us about." So the shepherds left their sheep and hurried to Bethlehem.

When they found the stable, they went in and saw Jesus lying in the manger and they were glad! Then they went back to their sheep in the field and told other people what the angel had told them about Jesus.

1. Why did men have to stay out in the fields with the sheep?
2. On the night Jesus was born, who came down from heaven to tell the shepherds in the field?
3. What did the shepherds find in the stable?

You can find this story in your Bible in Luke 2:8-20.

3. The Wise Men Follow the Star

There were also some other men who went to see Jesus in Bethlehem. They were called wise men. These men knew a lot about the stars in the sky. They studied about stars. Sometimes they would even stay up all night looking at the stars, trying to learn all about them.

One night when they were looking up at the sky, they saw a new star. This star was different from all the stars they had ever seen before. God sent that star for the wise men to see so they would know that Jesus had been born.

As soon as they found out that Jesus had been born, they wanted to go see Him. They thought they would go and find Him, but they lived a long way from Bethlehem. They did not know where Jesus was. So the wise men went to the city where the king lived. They asked the king's wise men to help them find the baby Jesus. The king's men told them the baby was supposed to be born in Bethlehem. So the wise men left to go to Bethlehem.

But how would they find their way? God made the star they had seen in the sky move along so the wise men could follow it. It showed the way to Bethlehem. And they followed the star until it came to the house where Jesus was. When the wise men saw Jesus, they kneeled down on the ground and worshiped him. Then they took out some presents they had brought and gave them to Jesus. After this they went back to their own homes.

1. Who else besides the shepherds heard about Jesus being born?
2. What did they like to study?
3. What did they see in the sky one night that was different?
4. Why did God send the new star to the wise men?
5. Who told them where to find the baby Jesus?
6. What did they do when they saw Jesus?
7. What did they give to Jesus?

You can find this story in your Bible in Matthew 2:1-12.

4. The Baby Jesus Escapes

The wise men went to see the king of the country where Bethlehem was. The king was the person who everybody had to mind. But this king was very wicked. When he found out that baby Jesus was born in Bethlehem, he thought that Jesus would become a king who would try to take over as king of the country. This made him very angry. He sent some men to Bethlehem to kill all the little children who were there. He did this because he wanted to kill baby Jesus. And the men went to Bethlehem and killed the little children there, but they did not kill Jesus.

They did not kill Jesus because God sent an angel from heaven to tell Joseph that the men were coming. The angel came to Joseph while he was asleep, and told him in a dream to hurry and take Jesus and Mary away from Bethlehem.

Joseph got up in the middle of the night while it was still dark and no one could see him. He took the baby Jesus and Mary the baby's mother, and went away to another country where the king's men could not find them.

After a while the wicked king died. Then Joseph took Jesus and Mary back to their own land. And they went to live in a city called Nazareth. Jesus lived in Nazareth for many years until He grew up to be a man. But the people did not know He was God's Son, because no one had told them yet.

1. Was there a king in the country where Bethlehem was?
2. Did everyone have to mind the king?
3. What did the wicked king send some men to Bethlehem to do?

4. Who told Joseph to take Jesus and Mary and escape?
5. Where did he take them?
6. What happened to the wicked king after a while?
7. Where did Joseph take Jesus and Mary to live until Jesus grew up?

You can find this story in your Bible in Matthew 2:13-23.

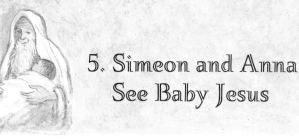

5. Simeon and Anna See Baby Jesus

While Jesus was still a baby, Mary and Joseph took Him to Jerusalem. Jerusalem was another city in the country they lived in. They took Him to the beautiful church there called the Temple. It was something every mother and father did with a new baby. They took the baby to the Temple so that He could be shown to the people and so they could dedicate Jesus to God. They also wanted the people to say a prayer for their new baby.

Now there was a man who lived in Jerusalem who loved God very much. His name was Simeon and he was an old man. He went to the Temple often so he could thank God and tell God how much he loved Him.

Now Simeon knew that God was going to send someone to help all the people one day. And God had promised Simeon that he would not die until he had seen this happen.

The day that Mary and Joseph went to the Temple to take baby Jesus, Simeon also went to the Temple. When he saw baby Jesus, he knew that this was God's special gift to His people. He knew Jesus was the special someone God had sent to help all people. Then he knew that God had kept His promise. He had let Simeon live long enough to see baby Jesus, God's Son.

When Simeon saw the baby, he held Him in his arms and prayed to God, thanking God for baby Jesus. Then he told Mary that Jesus would be an important person to the people in His land. He would grow up to help many people.

There was also a woman in the Temple that day. Her name was Anna and she was a widow. Her husband had died many years before and now she lived in the Temple where she prayed to God night and day. She was an old woman also and had spent much of her life waiting for God to send His Son.

When she saw baby Jesus, she knew that God had answered her prayers. She wanted everyone to know so she thanked God and began to tell others what she had seen in the Temple that day.

1. What was the name of the beautiful church in the city called Jerusalem?
2. Was Jesus a baby when Mary and Joseph took Him to the Temple?
3. Why did they take Him to the Temple?
4. What was the name of the old man who was in the Temple that day?
5. What was Simeon waiting for before he died?
6. Did Simeon know that baby Jesus was the special person God had sent to the world?
7. What was the name of the old woman in the Temple that day?
8. What did she do in the Temple day and night?
9. What did Anna tell everyone after she saw baby Jesus in the Temple?

You can find this story in your Bible in Luke 2:22-38.

6. Jesus Studies at the Temple

When Jesus was a boy, He grew up in Nazareth. But once a year Mary and Joseph and their family went to Jerusalem. They went for a special celebration called the feast of the Passover.

When Jesus was twelve years old, He went with His family to Jerusalem for the feast, as they did every year. When the feast was over, the family left to go back to Nazareth. But Jesus stayed behind in Jerusalem.

Now His parents did not know Jesus had stayed in Jerusalem. They traveled to Jerusalem and back with many other people, including relatives. So when they did not see Jesus near them, Mary and Joseph thought He was with some of His relatives or friends who were traveling back to Nazareth.

When they realized Jesus was not with any of the people traveling with them, they began to look for Him. They went back to Jerusalem and after three days, they found Jesus in the Temple. He was sitting with the teachers in the Temple, listening to them and asking them questions. The teachers in the Temple were surprised at how much the boy Jesus knew about God. They were amazed that such a young a boy knew so much about God.

When Mary came back to Jerusalem, she found Jesus with the teachers in the Temple. She told Jesus they had been very worried about Him when they did not find Him with the people they were traveling with. She asked Him why He had done this.

Jesus told His mother that He had to be in His Father's house. He said this because He knew that He was God's Son. And people went to the Temple to learn about God.

Then Jesus went with Mary and Joseph back to Nazareth. He always obeyed them. He lived there with his family until He grew up into a man.

1. How often did Mary and Joseph go to Jerusalem?
2. Why did they go to Jerusalem?
3. How old was Jesus when they went to the Passover feast in Jerusalem?
4. When they found Jesus was missing and looked for him, where did they find Him?
5. What was Jesus doing when they found Him?
6. Why did Jesus say He was in His Father's house?
7. Did Jesus obey His parents?

You can find this story in your Bible in Luke 2:41-52.

7. John the Baptist Tells About Jesus

There was a very good man in that country named John the Baptist. He did not live in the city where other people lived. He lived out in the wilderness, out in the fields and woods, where he could be all alone.

John wore a very strange coat. It was made of camel's hair. Camels are funny-looking animals. They have long necks and big humps on their backs. Their bodies are covered with hair. Some people cut off this hair and make clothes out of it. John the Baptist wore a coat that was made of camel's hair.

John did not eat the same food as you and I eat. He ate locusts and wild honey. Locusts are insects something like grasshoppers. They have wings and can fly.

John ate locusts, and he ate wild honey too. God made bees to make honey. Bees fly away to the flowers and take nectar from them. Then they carry it to their houses, called hives, and make the honey there.

There were bees out in the wilderness where John the Baptist lived. But they were wild bees, and they had no hives to live in because there was nobody out in the wilderness to make hives for them. So when they made honey, they went to holes in the trees and rocks and put the honey away there. And John the Baptist used to go and get the honey out of the trees and rocks and eat it.

John loved God and did everything God told him to do. One day God told John to leave the place in the wilderness. He told John to go and teach the people about Jesus and tell them that Jesus was God's Son, because it was time for the people to know about Jesus.

Then John went to a place near a river. It was called the river Jordan. And many people went to the Jordan River to hear what John would say. And John told the people that they would see Jesus very soon. He also told them they must get ready for Jesus to come to them.

And how were the people to get ready? The way to get ready for Jesus was to stop doing things that were wrong, and not do them anymore.

1. Where did John the Baptist live?
2. What did God tell John the Baptist to do?
3. What did John tell the people to do to get ready to see Jesus?

You can find this story in your Bible in Matthew 3:1-6 and Mark 1:2-6.

8. Jesus is Baptized

The people did what John the Baptist told them. They stopped doing wrong and promised to try not to do so anymore. Then John took the people down into the river Jordan and he baptized them in the river. This was so they could show others that they meant their promise about not doing wrong.

While John was baptizing the people, Jesus came and asked John to baptize Him. Then John took Jesus down into the river and baptized Him, too.

After Jesus was baptized He came up out of the water. And while He was coming up a very wonderful thing happened. He heard a voice speaking from the sky. It was God's voice. It said that Jesus was God's Son and that God loved Jesus and wanted all the people to obey Him.

And then a beautiful bird flew down from the sky. It looked like a dove. It came to Jesus and rested on Him. But it was not really a dove. It was the Holy Spirit who only looked like a dove. It was God's Spirit.

Then Jesus went out into the wilderness, where nobody lived. Only the wild animals were there. But the wild animals did not hurt Jesus because He was the Son of God, and God could keep them from hurting Jesus.

Jesus stayed out in the lonely wilderness with the wild animals for forty days and forty nights. All that time He did not eat any bread or drink any water. Afterwards, He was hungry.

1. Did the people listen to John the Baptist and do what he said?
2. What did John do to the people when he took them down to the river Jordan?
3. While John was baptizing the people, who came and asked to be baptized?

4. As Jesus came up out of the river, whose voice did He hear speaking from the sky?
5. What did the voice say?

6. What came flying from the sky after the voice spoke?
7. Was it really a dove or was it God's Holy Spirit?
8. Where did Jesus go after He was baptized?
9. How long did He stay in the wilderness?

You can find this story in your Bible in Matthew 3:13-17; Mark 1:9-11; Luke 3:21-22; and John 1:29-34.

9. Satan Tries to Make Jesus do Wrong

Now while Jesus was out in the wilderness, the bad spirit came there. His name is Satan. He came to try to make Jesus do wrong. Doing wrong is called sin.

Satan knew that Jesus was hungry. He had been in the wilderness without food or water for forty days and forty nights. So Satan told Jesus to change the stones that were lying on the ground into bread. Jesus could easily have changed the stones into bread. But He would not do it, because that would be obeying Satan.

Then Satan took Jesus away from the wilderness. He took him to a very high place on the top of a beautiful church called the Temple. Satan told Jesus to throw himself down from that high place. He said that God would send some angels to catch Him while he was falling, so that He would not be hurt when He fell.

But Jesus would not do this either, because to obey Satan would be wrong.

Then Satan took Jesus up to a very high hill, or mountain, and he showed Jesus many beautiful countries and beautiful cities from that high place. Jesus could see them all at the same time.

Satan told Jesus that if He would only obey him, Jesus could have all those beautiful countries and cities for His own. But Jesus said He would not obey Satan, but that He would obey God. Because God says in the Bible that He is the only one we should obey, or mind.

When Satan heard that Jesus would not mind him, Satan went away and left Jesus alone. Then God sent some good angels from heaven to help Jesus and to bring Him some food and water.

Sometimes Satan comes to us and tries to make us do wrong. We cannot see him when he comes, but we know he is near because he makes us feel as if we want to do wrong.

When we feel like that, we can tell Satan that

we will not do wrong. Then he will go away from us, just like he went away from Jesus. God will help us and give us the good things we need.

1. Who came out into the wilderness to try to make Jesus do wrong?
2. What did Satan tell Jesus to turn the stones into?
3. Could Jesus have changed the stones into bread?
4. But would he do it to obey Satan?
5. Who did Satan say would come and catch Jesus if He threw Himself off the top of the temple?
6. Did Jesus do what Satan said?
7. What did Satan show Jesus from the top of the mountain.
8. Who did Jesus obey?
9. Does Satan ever try to make us do wrong?
10. Can we see him when he comes?
11. What should we say to Satan when he tries to make us do wrong?

You can find this story in your Bible in Matthew 4:1-11; Mark 1:12-13; and Luke 4:1-13.

10. Jesus Goes to a Wedding

Jesus traveled to a city. Remember that a city is a place where there are a lot of houses and a lot of people. The city Jesus came into was called Cana. A man in that city had just been married, and this man invited many people to his house to celebrate. They were having a wedding feast, or great meal. There was good food on the table to eat and wine for them to drink.

Wine is made out of grapes. Many grapes grew in the country where Cana was and the people used them to make wine. And the man who had been married put some wine on his table for his friends to drink at the feast.

But so many people came to the party that there was not enough for everyone to drink.

Jesus was also invited to this wedding party.

When He heard that there was no more wine, He found the servants. They were the people who brought the food and wine out to the guests at the table. He told them to bring in some water and to pour the water into some larger pitchers or jars that were in the room. There were six jars standing around on the floor of the room where they were having the meal. These were very big jars made out of stone.

So the servants did as Jesus said. They brought in water and poured it into the jars, filling them all up to the top. Then Jesus told them to take out some of the water and give it to the man who was serving at the head of the table.

So the servants took some of the water in a cup and handed it to the man and he tasted it. He found out that it was not water anymore. It was wine! Jesus had made the water in the jars turn into wine.

Jesus did not touch the water or put anything in it. He just told the servants to take some out and when they did, it was wine. This happened because Jesus is the Son of God.

When Jesus changed the water into wine, it was a miracle. A miracle is something that happens but you cannot explain how. You cannot do a miracle and I cannot do a miracle. But Jesus can do a miracle, because He is the Son of God and He can do the same things God can do.

1. What was the man who got married doing for his friends who came to his house?
2. What was on the table for the feast?
3. What did Jesus tell the servants to fill the jars with?
4. What is a miracle?
5. Who can do miracles? Why?

You can find this story in your Bible in John 2:1-11.

11. Jesus Heals the Rich Man's Son

Jesus went again to the city called Cana where He had changed the water into wine. There was a rich man in that city, and this man had a son who was very sick. No doctor could cure him and no medicine could make him well. His father was afraid his son would die.

Now this rich man had heard about Jesus being at the wedding feast. And he had heard all about Jesus turning the water into wine. He thought if Jesus could do that, He could help his son become well again.

So when the rich man heard Jesus was in Cana again, he went to Jesus and begged Him to make his son well. He said, "Come quickly, before my son dies." He was afraid his son would die before Jesus could get back to his house. He thought that Jesus could not cure the boy until He went to the man's home and saw his son. Then he hoped Jesus could do something to make his son well.

But Jesus did not go with the man. Instead, he told the rich man to go back to his home. "Your son will get well," Jesus said to him.

The man believed what Jesus said and he started back for his home. But before he could get there, some people from his house came and found him. And they told him some wonderful news. His son had gotten well!

The man was so happy about his son. He had been so afraid his son might die.

Jesus had cured the man's son just by saying he would be well. He did not even have to go to see the boy. As soon as Jesus had said it, the boy's sickness went away and he was well. This was another miracle, like Jesus' turning the water into wine.

1. What was wrong with the rich man's son?
2. Could any doctor or medicine make him better?
3. Did the man think Jesus should go to his house to cure his son?
4. What did Jesus say to the man?
5. Who made the man's son well?

You can find this story in your Bible in John 4:46-54.

12. Jesus Has to Leave Nazareth

As Jesus traveled on, He came to the city of Nazareth. Remember, this was the city where He lived with Mary His mother and Joseph His father when He was a little boy. There was a church in Nazareth. The people in town went to the church each week to hear about God. Just like you go to church on Sunday, the people went to their church. Only the day they went to church was called the Sabbath Day. But it was the last day of the week instead of the first.

On the Sabbath Day Jesus went into the church in Nazareth and there were many people there. They had come to hear about God.

Jesus told the people in the church that God had sent Him to teach them. But the people were not happy with Jesus, even though they had watched Him grow up as a boy in their city. They would not believe that God had sent Jesus Jesus.

The people were so unhappy when they heard Jesus that they became angry with Him. So they took Him and led Him out of the church to the top of a steep hill near their city. They wanted to throw Jesus down off the hill and even kill Him because of what He had said. They did not believe Him and they wanted to hurt Him.

But Jesus was the Son of God and they could not hurt Him. He could even keep them from hurting Him. So He got away from them and left Nazareth, the city where He grew up.

Jesus decided not to teach the people of that church any more because they would not listen to Him or believe that God had sent Him to teach them. So Jesus left His home town.

1. What was the name of the town where Jesus had lived as a boy?
2. Where did Jesus go to teach the people in Nazareth?
3. What day did the people go to the church to learn about God?
4. What day is that like when you go to your church?
5. What did Jesus tell the people in the church?
6. What did they think when Jesus told them that God had sent Him to teach them?
7. What did they want to do to Jesus when they got angry?
8. Were they able to hurt Jesus?
9. Why could they not hurt Jesus?
10. What did Jesus do when He got away from the people who were trying to hurt Him?

You can find this story in your Bible in Luke 4:16-30; Matthew 13:53-58; and Mark 6:1-6.

13. Jesus Goes Fishing

Jesus came to another city called Capernaum. This city was beside a big lake. Jesus walked along the shore of the lake and talked to the people. Many people had heard of His miracles and they followed Him.

Jesus saw two fishing boats on the shore. They belonged to men who sailed out to catch fish. When Jesus saw the boats, the men were fixing their nets. These nets were made of rope and were used to catch fish. Sometimes the nets would get big holes in them and the fishermen would mend them.

When the people crowded around Jesus to hear Him, He got into one of the boats and told the man who owned the boat to push it out a little way into the water. Jesus sat down in the boat and talked to the people on the shore.

When He finished talking to the people, He told the man to sail out onto the lake and catch some fish. The man said he and his brother had tried all night to catch some fish, but they had not caught any. Still, he said he would try again. This man's name was Peter.

So Peter and his brother Andrew rowed their boat out onto the lake and let their net down. When they tried to pull it up again, it was so full of fish they could not pull it up by themselves.

Then Peter called some other fishermen to help them. These men rowed out in their boat to help Peter and Andrew pull in their net full of fish. They put all the fish in the two boats, and the boats were so full that they were almost ready to sink.

It was Jesus who made the fish come together. Jesus made so many fish come that both boats were filled up.

This was a miracle, like changing the water into wine. Jesus did this miracle so these men would know that Jesus was the Son of God.

Afterwards, Jesus told the men to come with Him. They left their boats, their nets, their fish, and all that they had and they went with Jesus.

After that, these men stayed with Jesus and traveled with Him as His helpers.

1. Jesus saw two things on the shore—what were they?
2. After Jesus finished teaching the people, what did He tell the man in the boat to do?
3. What was the man's name?
4. What happened when they put their fish nets out again as Jesus told them to do?
5. When Jesus asked the men to come with Him, what did they do?

You can find this story in your Bible in Luke 5:1-11; Matthew 4:18-22; and Mark 1:16-20.

14. Jesus Heals Peter's Mother-in-law

After Jesus met Peter and his brother Andrew, He stayed a little while in Capernaum where He had met them by the large lake. Peter and Andrew lived in that city and Peter's mother-in-law, his wife's mother, lived with Peter.

Jesus went to the house where Peter lived. Peter's mother-in-law was lying on her bed. She was very sick. She had a high fever. Peter and the others asked Jesus to help her and to make her well. They had seen His miracle with the fish and believed He could help the sick woman.

Jesus went to the woman and stood by the bed where she lay with a high fever. Jesus told the fever to go away from her, and the fever went away. Then Jesus took her hand and held it and raised her up out of the bed. And she was well!

She felt so much better that she got up from her bed and fixed something to eat for all the people who were in the house.

Later that day in the evening, the sun was going down and it began to get dark. By this time, many people in the city had heard how Jesus had healed Peter's mother-in-law. Maybe they also had seen Jesus' miracle with the fish on the lake. They all believed Jesus could help other people they knew who weren't well. So the people in the city brought their sick friends to Jesus and He cured them all outside Peter's house. Many people were healed and each time it was a miracle. Then Jesus stayed all night at Peter's house.

1. Whose house did Jesus go to in Capernaum?
2. Was there a sick woman in this house? Who was she? What was wrong with her?
3. What did Peter and his friends ask Jesus to do for her?
4. When Jesus told the fever to go away, what happened?
5. That evening, as it began to get dark, who did other people bring to Jesus?

You can find this story in your Bible in Matthew 8:14-16; Mark 1:29-34; and Luke 4:38-41.

15. Jesus Prays and Decides to Leave

After Jesus spent the night at Peter's house, He got up very early the next morning. It was so early the sun was not yet up in the sky. Jesus rose from His bed, left the house, and walked out of the city out into the wilderness. Remember, the wilderness is a place where no people live, out in the fields and woods. When He got to where He could be alone, Jesus kneeled down on the ground and prayed to God.

Jesus knew that He was God's Son. God had sent Jesus to earth to teach people about Him and how much He loved them. Jesus knew the people had been crowding around Him to hear Him teach and to be made well. He wanted to help all the people, but He also knew He had to have some time by Himself to think so He could help them more. He knew God had sent Him, so He knew God would help Him when he prayed to God. This is why he went out early in the morning to be alone. He needed to talk to God, His Father.

But after Jesus had gone out into the wilderness outside the city, the people in the city came to Peter's house to find Jesus. When they heard He had gone out into the wilderness, they went out to find Him.

They found Jesus where He was and begged Him to stay in their city for a while. They wanted to spend more time with Jesus.

But Jesus said He had to leave Capernaum. He had to go because there were other people who needed Him, too. There were people in other cities in that country who Jesus wanted to teach about God.

So Jesus left Capernaum with Peter and Andrew and His other helpers. He called his helpers "disciples." He called them this because a disciple is like a student. It is someone who listens to a teacher and follows what that teacher tells him. These helpers were men who listened to Jesus and stayed with Him. So they were called disciples.

Jesus and His disciples went into the other cities and began to teach the people who lived there about God. Jesus told them they needed to repent. To repent means to be sorry for the things you do that are wrong. Jesus meant that the people should be sorry for their sins.

The people's sins were the bad things they had done. Jesus wanted them to be sorry for these things and not do them anymore.

1. Where did Jesus go very early in the morning, before the sun was up in the sky?
2. Why did Jesus have to go out of the city into the wilderness to be alone?
3. What did Jesus do when He came out in the wilderness?
4. Who went out into the wilderness to find Jesus?
5. When they found Jesus, what did they ask Him to do?
6. Did Jesus say He must go to other cities and teach the people who lived there, too?
7. Who left with Jesus to go to the other cities?
8. What is a disciple?
9. Did Jesus go to the other cities to tell the people about God?
10. Did Jesus tell the people to repent?
11. What does repent mean?
12. What were the people to be sorry for?
13. What are our sins?
14. Does Jesus tell us we must be sorry for our sins and not do them any more?

You can find this story in your Bible in Mark 1:35-38 and Luke 4:42-43.

16. Jesus Heals the Leper

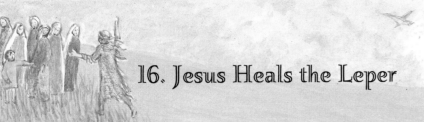

Sometimes the people in that land sometimes used to get a very bad sickness. It was a disease called leprosy. Leprosy made people have bad sores all over their skin. It made their skin look very pale.

When a person got leprosy, he had to go away from his home to live by himself in some other place. Sometimes he would live with other people who had to leave their homes because they had leprosy, too. If the people who had leprosy stayed at home, their families might get leprosy, too, because it is a sickness that other people can get from someone who has it.

After the person with leprosy had left his home, he could never go back until he was well. And leprosy was a sickness that no one knew how to cure. Only God could make a person well who had leprosy.

One day a man who had leprosy came to Jesus. A person with leprosy was called a leper. This leper saw Jesus and kneeled down on the ground before Him. This was a brave thing to do. When most people saw lepers coming, they ran away because they did not want to get leprosy. The man hoped that Jesus would not run away from him. And as he kneeled in front of Jesus, he asked Jesus to make him well.

Jesus was sorry for the poor man and said to him, "I will do it. Be well." As soon as Jesus had spoken these words, the leprosy went away from the man. His skin was all clean with no sores and he was well. This was a miracle, because leprosy was a sickness no one knew how to cure. But Jesus made the leper well.

The man was so happy that he went out into his city and told all the people how Jesus had cured him. After that, so many people came to Jesus and crowded around Him that He could not stay in that city any longer.

1. What very bad sickness did people used to have in the land where Jesus lived?
2. When a person had leprosy, did he have to go away and live by himself until he was well?

3. Why could he not live at home?
4. Could anybody make him well but God?
5. Did Jesus run away when the man with leprosy came to him?
6. What did the man with leprosy ask Jesus to do for him?
7. Did Jesus make the man well?
8. What did the man do after this?

You can find this story in your Bible in Matthew 8:1-4; Mark 1:40-45, and Luke 5:12-16.

17. Jesus Heals a Man Who Could Not Walk

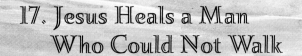

After Jesus healed the leper, He went again to Capernaum. The houses in that city did not have two or three stories like homes we might live in. They were low houses, only one story high. And the roofs on these houses were not pointed. The roofs on these houses were flat, so that people could go up on the roof and walk around. The roofs were made of grass and clay.

Jesus went into one of these houses. People heard that Jesus had returned to their city and remembered that He had cured many people when He had visited before. So the people began to bring their sick friends to Jesus.

Some people had a friend who was so sick he could not walk or stand up. He was paralyzed. If someone is paralyzed, that person cannot move his legs. This man had to lie on his bed, which was like a mattress on the floor.

The sick man's friends heard that Jesus was in town so they took the man to Jesus. They had to carry the man to Jesus on his bed.

But when they got to the house where Jesus was, there were so many people that they could not get their friend in the door. So many people had come to hear Jesus there was no room for anyone else. How could they get the man into the house when he could not walk?

Do you know what these men did? They took the mattress he was lying on and they carried him on his bed up to the roof. Then they made a hole in the roof and they lowered the man down on his bed into the room below, where Jesus was.

When Jesus saw how much trouble they had taken to bring the sick man to Him, He was glad. He said to the man, "Stand up on your feet, and take up your bed and carry it to your home." When Jesus said this to him, the man became well.

Before Jesus spoke to him he could not stand up at all. But now he could could pick up his mattress and carry it! When the people saw the man do this they were surprised, and said to one another, "We have seen a wonderful thing today!"

1. After Jesus went into one of these houses, who did some men bring to see Him?
2. What was wrong with the man?
3. Where did the men take their friend to get him into the house?
4. What did Jesus tell the man to do?

You can find this story in your Bible in Mark 2:1-12; Luke 5:17-26; and Matthew 9:1-8.

18. Jesus Heals a Man at the Pool

In the city of Jerusalem was a little pond, or pool of water, called the Pool of Bethesda.

Sometimes the water in the pool moved on its own, like someone had gotten into the pool. They thought it was an angel who went into the pool and moved the water. They thought that if a sick person was the first one to go into the water when it moved, the sick person would get well.

So a lot of people stayed by this pool. Some of them were blind and others were lame. Some of them were sick and weak. They were all waiting for the water to move, so that they could go down into it quickly and be made well.

On the Sabbath Day, which is like Sunday , Jesus went to this pool. He saw all the sick people waiting there by the water. One of them was a man who had been sick for thirty-eight years. Jesus knew how long it had been, because He knows everything about us.

This man was lying on his bed and could not get up to get down into the pool. So Jesus spoke to him and asked, "Would you like to be made well?" The man said that he would, but when the water moved he had no one to help him get into the pool. Before he could get there, someone else stepped into the pool and he was too late.

Then Jesus said to him, "Stand up and take up your bed and walk." At once the man was able to do what Jesus told him. He stood up, picked up his bed and carried it. He was well!

When the man told other people Jesus had healed him, some of them became angry. Jesus had cured the man on the Sabbath Day. The people had a rule in those days that no one was to do any work on the Sabbath Day. But Jesus had healed a man and some of the people thought it was like doing work.

But Jesus told them that God had sent Him to make sick people well. He said that He could not only make sick people well, but dead people become alive again. Jesus also told them that a day was coming when He would make all people who were dead come alive again. Jesus called this day the Judgment Day.

1. Why did the people think an angel came and got into the pool?
2. Why did many sick people wait by the pool?
3. How long had the man who Jesus spoke to been sick?
4. What did Jesus tell him to do?
5. Who did Jesus say had sent Him to make sick people well?

You can find this story in your Bible in John 5:2-47.

19. Jesus Tells a Story About a Sheep

Jesus went into a church on the Sabbath Day, like our Sunday, and a lot of people were there. One of the men had something wrong with his hand. He could not open and close his hand like you can. His hand was stiff and curled up like it was dead. He could hardly use his hand at all.

Because this man could not use his hand, he could not work to earn money to buy food for his little children. So when Jesus saw the man, He wanted to help him. He told the man to stand up in the church where all the people there could see him. Jesus told the man to stand up because He was going to make his hand well.

But some men in the church did not like this. Remember when the people in Jerusalem were angry with Jesus because he made a man well on the Sabbath Day? Well, this was also a Sabbath Day. The men said Jesus should not make the man well on that day because they said God told them not to work on the Sabbath Day.

Then Jesus said to these men, "Suppose you had a sheep out in the field, and it fell into a deep hole, called a pit, on a Sabbath Day. Would you go and lift it up out of the pit?" Jesus knew the men would say yes because they would want to take care of their animals. If a sheep fell in a big hole and could not get out, it might die or be hurt badly if no one got it out when it fell.

Then Jesus told the men that if they would be kind to their sheep and take care of it on the Sabbath Day, shouldn't they also be kind to this man with the bad hand? So Jesus taught the men who were angry with Him that it is right to be kind to persons who are poor and sick, even on the Sabbath Day.

Then Jesus said to the man, "Stretch out your hand."

At once the man's hand was made well, and he

could stretch it out like the other.

Before that time the man could not move his hand at all. But Jesus had made it strong and well by speaking those few words. And now the man could go and work and earn food for his little children to eat.

1. Where did Jesus go on the Sabbath Day?
2. Was a man there who had something wrong with his hand?
3. Why did the man's hurt hand keep him from feeding his children?
4. Why did some men in the church think Jesus should not cure the man right then?
5. What did Jesus ask them they would do if their sheep fell in a hole on the Sabbath Day?
6. Should we help people who are poor and sick no matter what day it is?
7. What did Jesus then say to the man with the bad hand?
8. What happened to the man's hand after Jesus spoke these words?
9. What was the man able to do for his children after Jesus made his hand well?

You can find this story in your Bible in Matthew 12:9-14; Mark 3:1-6; and Luke 6:6-11.

20. Jesus Teaches His Disciples

After this, Jesus went out into the lonely wilderness and stayed there all night praying to God. In the morning He called twelve of the men who had been traveling with Him. He chose these twelve men to stay with Him all the time. These included Peter and Andrew.

Jesus chose these men to help Him while He went about teaching people the things God wanted them to know. These twelve men were to do whatever Jesus told them to do, and to go wherever He told them to go.

These twelve men were called disciples. Remember that disciples are those who listen to a teacher and do what that teacher says.

Jesus went up on a mountain and His disciples followed him there. Then they sat down and a big crowd of people came to Jesus so He could teach them. Jesus taught the people what they must do to please God.

He said they must not be proud and think of themselves as being too good. To be proud means to think you are better than other people. Instead, they should remember how often they had done wrong and they must be sorry for doing it.

Jesus also told the people they must be kind to each other. Sometimes people are mean to each other and hurt each other's feelings. But God is not pleased when they do this.

Jesus also said they must not fight with each other or have arguments. He also said they must not be angry with each other. When someone was unkind to them, they must not be unkind in return. Instead, they should be kind to that person and pray for him.

Jesus also told the people they must try all the time to mind what God said. God created us all and He knows what we need. He also knows how much happier we would be if we would treat each other kindly. God does not want any one treated unkindly, not even animals. He loves all people very much. So He wanted Jesus to tell the people how to live so they could get along with each other and love each other like He loves them.

1. How should people treat each other?
2. Why does God want people to be kind to one another?
3. If someone is unkind to us, should we be unkind to them?

You can find this story in your Bible in Matthew 5:1-12; Mark 3:7-12; and Luke 6:17-23.

21. Jesus Heals the Soldier's Servant

Jesus again went to visit the city of Capernaum. A man lived there who was a soldier. Soldiers worked for the people who ruled the country. The soldier's job was to take care of the city and to keep bad things from happening in the city.

This soldier had a servant who he loved very much. A servant was a person who lived with someone all the time and who took care of all the things that might need to be done in the house.

This soldier's servant was very sick. Because the soldier loved him so dearly he did not want the servant to die.

And so the soldier came to see Jesus. He had heard about Jesus making people well. He wanted to see if Jesus could help his sick servant. So he found Jesus and asked Him to make his servant well.

The soldier may have heard that Jesus had made people well without even touching them, and sometimes without even being with them. So the soldier said that Jesus did not need to go see his servant, or give him any medicine, or do anything to make him well. All he wanted Jesus to do was to say the servant would get well. Then the soldier was sure he would get well.

Jesus was pleased with the soldier for thinking He could make his servant well by only telling him to be well. So Jesus told the soldier to go back to his home, because his servant would get well.

Then the soldier went back to his home. When he got there, he found that his servant was no longer sick. Jesus had made him well!

1. When Jesus went into the city of Capernaum, who came to see Him there?
2. What is a servant?
3. Did the soldier love his servant very much?
4. What was wrong with his servant?
5. Did the soldier want Jesus to make his servant well?

6. How did the soldier think Jesus could make his servant well?
7. Was Jesus pleased with the soldier for believing in Him?
8. When the soldier went home, what did he find?

You can find this story in your Bible in Matthew 8:5-13 and Luke 7:1-10.

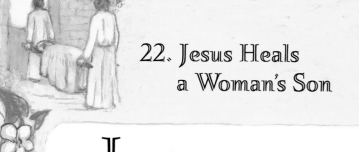

22. Jesus Heals a Woman's Son

Jesus went to a city called Nain. This city had a high wall built around it and there was a gate in the wall for the people to go through whenever they went in and out of the city.

As Jesus came near the city, He met some men coming out of the gate. They were carrying a man on a small platform. This platform was called a *bier*. It was a platform to carry a person who had died to the graveyard. Today we use something like this called a coffin.

The men Jesus met were carrying a dead man out to his grave to bury him. The man was the only son his mother had. His mother was also a widow because her husband had died earlier. Now she was walking with the others as they carried her son to his grave. She was crying because she knew she would never see him again. She loved him very much and would miss him.

When Jesus saw her crying, He felt sorry for her and told her not to cry. Then He walked up to the platform holding her dead son and He touched it. The men who carried it stood still.

Jesus spoke to the dead man and said, "Young man, I say to you, arise." He told a man who was dead to get up! As soon as Jesus had spoken these words, the dead man became alive again. He sat up and began to talk. And Jesus gave the mother back her only son.

When the crowd of people who were there saw the dead man come to life, they were afraid. They had never seen anything like that before. It was scary to see a man who was dead suddenly sit up and talk because he was alive again. But even though they were afraid, they also knew that God had sent Jesus to them. Because if God had not sent Him, Jesus could not do such a wonderful thing as bring a dead person to life again.

1. When Jesus came near to the city, who was being carried out of the gate?
2. Where were they taking this man?
3. Was the dead man the only son his mother had?

4. When Jesus saw her crying, what did He tell her?
5. What did Jesus say to the dead man?
6. What happened then?
7. How did the people feel when they saw the dead man come to life again?
8. Who did they say had sent Jesus to them?

You can find this story in your Bible in Luke 7:11-17.

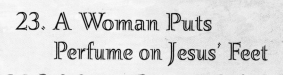

23. A Woman Puts Perfume on Jesus' Feet

The people in the country where Jesus lived used to have something like perfume or lotion. It was called *ointment.* They would rub it on their hair and on their skin. This ointment would make their skin feel very soft and smooth, and it had a very sweet smell, like perfume. This ointment also cost a lot of money.

One day while Jesus was visiting a town, a man asked Jesus to come to his house. Jesus went to the man's house with some of His disciples, or helpers, and they sat down to eat dinner. While they were eating, a woman came into the room. She was holding a little jar in her hand. The jar was full of sweet-smelling ointment.

The woman broke open the jar and poured the ointment on Jesus' feet. Then she kneeled down in front of Jesus and kissed His feet and wiped them with her long hair. She did this because she wanted to show how much she loved Jesus. The ointment was the most special thing she owned. And she loved Jesus so much she wanted to give it to Him. She loved Jesus because He had come down from heaven to be her Savior.

What is a Savior? If someone were to rescue you from a fire or from some scary animal, that person would save you from a scary place and take you to a safe place. Jesus is like that. He comes to save us from our sins, from the bad things we do. The woman knew Jesus had come to save her from her sins, too.

She had often done wrong and made God angry with her, but now she was sorry for it. And Jesus said He would forgive her. This means He would excuse the bad things she had done so God would not be angry with her any more and she would not be punished for what she had done wrong.

Because Jesus did this, He was her Savior and the woman wanted to thank Jesus. But some of

the disciples did not like the woman coming in and putting the ointment on Jesus' feet because it was an expensive ointment. Jesus told them to leave her alone because she was showing how much she loved Him.

1. What did the people in Jesus' time put on their hair and their skin?
2. While Jesus was eating dinner, who came into the room where He was?
3. What did she do with the ointment in the jar?

You can find this story in your Bible in Matthew 26:6-13; Mark 14:3-9; and Luke 7:36-50.

24. Jesus Heals a Blind Man

One day some people brought a man to see Jesus. The man was blind and could not see. He also was mute, which meant he could not speak. Other people could see the sun shining and the flowers growing. Other people could see their friends' faces and could talk with their friends and their families.

But this man could not see his friends or family. He could not talk with them. He could hear them speak to him, but he could not answer them. He also could not enjoy the beautiful world around him or sing a song. And he could not go anywhere without someone helping him.

When Jesus saw this man in the city, He felt sorry for him. So Jesus made him well. How happy the man must have been when he opened his eyes and found that he could see and when he opened his mouth and found he could speak. Now he could talk with his friends and family, whom he loved. And he could look around at the flowers, trees, and birds and see the faces of those he loved.

The man thanked Jesus and Jesus was happy knowing that He had been able to do a miracle and make this man well.

1. What was the matter with the man who was brought to Jesus?
2. Could this man see his friends when they came to him, or answer them when they spoke to him?
3. Did Jesus feel sorry for the man when He saw him?
4. What did He do to help the man?
5. What could the man do after Jesus made him well?
6. What are your favorite things to see?
7. How do you like to use your voice to speak or to sing?
8. Do you think the man loved Jesus for being so kind to him?

You can find this story in your Bible in Matthew 12:22-23.

25. Jesus Tells About a Man with Many Barns

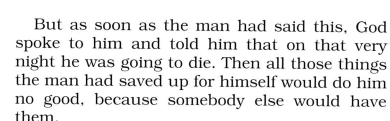

Sometimes when Jesus taught the people who came to hear Him, He would use stories to teach them about God. One day He told the people around him about a man who had a lot of good things to eat and to drink. He was rich and owned a lot of things.

Because the man had so many good things, he built some large buildings called barns. Inside these barns he put all these good things away to save them up for himself.

Then after he had put all the things away, he said to himself, "Now I have everything I want. I do not need to work any more, so I will do whatever I want to, whatever pleases me. Then I will have a nice time as long as I live."

But as soon as the man had said this, God spoke to him and told him that on that very night he was going to die. Then all those things the man had saved up for himself would do him no good, because somebody else would have them.

After Jesus had told this story, He said that we should not be like that man who built many barns to hold all the things he had. All that man cared about was getting rich and doing what would please himself. He did not think of other people and what they needed. He did not think of pleasing God.

Jesus did not mean we should not have things. What He meant was that we should share what we have. Whatever we have is ours to meet our needs and to help others who might not have as much. We must learn to thank God for all the things we have, and remember that God did not give them to us to store away so others could not get them. He gives us good things because he loves us and we must share with others to show them how much God loves them, too.

We must want to please God instead of always wanting to please ourselves. When we share what we have, it pleases God.

1. What did the man in this story have?
2. What did the man put away in his barns?
3. After he had put away all his good things there, what did he say to himself?
4. After he said this, what did God say to the man?
5. Who gives us the good things we have?

You can find this story in your Bible in Luke 12:16-21.

26. Jesus Talks About God's Love

One day Jesus was speaking to a crowd of people on the side of a mountain. They had gathered to hear Jesus teach. He was teaching them how to live in ways that would please God.

Jesus began to teach them about how God takes care of those He loves. Jesus told the people not to worry. When we worry, we are thinking too much about what might happen to us. Worrying also means being afraid of not having what we need. We might wonder if we will have enough food to eat or if we will have clothes to wear. When we worry, we are not believing that God will take care of us.

So Jesus told the people not to worry about their lives, because God would always take care of them and give them food to eat and clothes to wear.

Then Jesus pointed to some birds in a tree and to some flowers on the ground. He said the birds and the flowers were a good example of not worrying about things. The birds fly in the air and do not collect food in barns or plant food to eat, but God gives them food to eat. They do not worry about it. And the flowers do not worry about what they will wear because God made them beautiful for all people to enjoy.

So if God takes care of the birds and flowers He made, He will also take care of the people He loves. God gave the little birds food to eat, Jesus said, and God cares more for the people who love Him than He does for the little birds.

So if we love and obey Jesus, we do not need to worry or to be afraid. God will never forget us, and He will always watch over us.

1. When Jesus was teaching the people, what did He tell them about worry?
2. What does it mean to worry about something?
3. What did Jesus use as an example of how God takes care of us?
4. What does God give to the birds?
5. Does God care more about the people He loves than He does for the little birds?
6. Did Jesus say God would always give the people who love and obey Him food to eat and clothes to wear?
7. If we love and obey Jesus, do we need to be afraid that God will forget us?

You can find this story in your Bible in Matthew 6:25-34 and Luke 12:22-32.

27. Jesus Talks About Sowing Seeds

Jesus told a story about a man who went out into the field to plant wheat. Wheat is what bread is made of. It comes from little grains that grow on tall branches called stalks. If we take these grains of wheat and plant them, they will grow up and make more wheat for bread.

So Jesus told a story about a man who went out to a field to plant wheat. The way he did this was to take grains in his hand and scatter them over the ground.

But some of the grains fell in the wrong place. The birds saw them, and they flew down and ate them up. So these grains of wheat were wasted.

Some of the other grains fell in a place where there were a lot of rocks and stones on the ground. Some others fell where weeds grew. These grains of wheat could not grow either, because the stones and the weeds would not give the wheat room to grow.

But the rest of the grains that the man scattered fell in the right place. They fell where the ground was soft and ready. Then the rain came and the sun shone and the grains grew little roots in the ground and grew up. After a while, they made more wheat for the man than he had first carried out in the field and planted.

This is the way it is when children are learning what Jesus wants them to do. Some of them do not listen to their teachers or to what their parents say. And then it is just as if something took away the words their parents spoke, and the children do not remember them.

Some of the children remember the words they hear about Jesus, but other things become more important so they do not pay attention to the words about Jesus. This is just like when the weeds and stones did not give the seeds enough room to be grow.

But some children listen to the words they hear

about Jesus and they try to obey what Jesus says. They are like the wheat that fell on the good ground and grew up to make more wheat for the man who planted it. When we listen to what Jesus says, and then obey it, we please God. Then we might show someone else how to please God.

1. What was the man planting in his field?
2. How did the man in the field plant the wheat?
3. What flew down from the trees and ate them up?
4. When you listen and obey what Jesus says, is it like the wheat that fell on the good places?

You can find this story in your Bible in Matthew 13:1-23; Mark 4:1-20; and Luke 8:4-15.

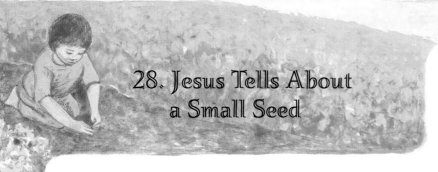

28. Jesus Tells About a Small Seed

Have you ever planted a seed? You know that seeds are what flowers, vegetables, and even trees grow from.

One day Jesus told the people about a small seed. This particular seed was a mustard seed. There are many different kinds of seeds that we plant in the ground to make things grow. Some seeds are large and some are small. The mustard seed is a tiny seed. It is not much larger than the head of a pin.

The mustard seed is so small that if you were holding one in your hand and you dropped it, you would hardly be able to see it or find it again.

But even though the mustard seed is small, when it is planted in the ground, it grows up to be a tree. It grows into a tree large enough for birds to stand on its branches and to make their nest in it.

Now if you were to look at a mustard seed before planting it in the ground, you might think it would be impossible for a seed so tiny to grow into a tree. But God turns that tiny seed into a place for birds to come and rest and sing.

When Jesus told the people about the mustard seed, he compared it to loving God. When children like you begin to love Jesus, their love is like a tiny mustard seed before it is planted in the ground. It seems very small at first. But if they keep on listening to what Jesus says and obeying Him, then their love will grow bigger and bigger. It will grow like the mustard seed grows up into a tree.

1. What is a seed?
2. What kind of a seed did Jesus tell the people about?
3. Is the mustard seed big or small?
4. When it is planted in the ground, what does it grow up to be?
5. When little children first begin to love Jesus, is their love small like a mustard seed?
6. If they keep on trying to obey Jesus, does their love for Jesus grow bigger and bigger?
7. How is this like the mustard seed?

You can find this story in your Bible in Matthew 13:31-32; Mark 4:30-32; and Luke 13:18-19.

29. Jesus Tells About a Woman Making Bread

Jesus told another story about a woman making some bread for her family. Have you ever seen someone making bread dough? First, the woman takes some white flour and puts some water in it. Then she works it with her hands and makes it into dough.

But she also does something else to turn the dough into bread. She takes a cup and puts something called yeast in the cup. Then she pours a little yeast into the dough. After she does this, she covers the dough and leaves it alone. This little bit of yeast makes the dough puff up so that it will make a nice loaf of bread. The yeast makes the dough better than before. This way, when it is put in the oven and baked, it makes a better-tasting bread.

Without the little bit of yeast, the bread would be hard and flat and would not taste as good. It only takes a little bit of yeast to mix with the flour and water to spread throughout all the bread dough. God's love is like the yeast. It spreads out to all people everywhere.

When Jesus told this story, He was telling the people about loving God. When little children love God, it makes them better children than they were before. If they love God, then they want to do the right things to please God, because they know how much God loves them, too.

1. What was the woman doing in the story Jesus told the people?
2. After the woman poured water into the flour to make dough, what else did she put in the dough?
3. When children love God, does that make them better children than they were before?

You can find this story in your Bible in Matthew 13:33 and Luke 13:20-21.

30. Jesus Tells About a Big Pearl

Jesus told the people a story about a man who wanted to buy some pearls. Pearls are beautiful little white stones. Sometimes we see pearls in rings, bracelets, and earrings. Where do you think pearls come from? They come from under the water. They come from way down under the ocean.

People swim down under the ocean and find oysters on the bottom of the sea. Then they bring these oysters up on the land, open them, and sometimes find pearls inside them. Then they take out the pearls and sell them.

Once there was a man who wanted to buy some pearls. He did not want to swim down under the water to find them for himself. He wanted to buy them from the men who had found them already. So he went to these men and asked them to show him all the pearls they had to sell.

At last one of the men showed him a very beautiful pearl. It was larger and prettier than any pearl he had ever seen before. But it would cost so much that he did not have enough money to buy it. So he told the man to keep that pearl until he came back again. Then he went away and sold everything he had to get enough money to buy that beautiful pearl.

Perhaps the man had a house and land, some horses, cows and sheep. But he sold them all and got money for them. Then he went back to the man and gave him the money and bought the beautiful pearl. Then he was very happy, because he had the thing he wanted more than anything else in the world.

What should we want more than anything else in this world? Not a pearl, for that will not make us happy. We should want God to be pleased with us, and we should want Him to take us to be His children.

We should want this as much as the man wanted the beautiful pearl. We should be willing to do everything God tells us to do, and to stop doing the things He tells us not to do. This will please God and will also make us very happy.

1. What is a pearl?
2. Where do you see pearls today?
3. Where do pearls come from?
4. What did the man in the story want to buy?
5. When he saw the most beautiful pearl, why did he not buy it right away?
6. What did the man do, so that he would have enough money to buy the pearl?
7. How did he feel when he got the pearl he wanted so much?
8. Did he want the pearl more than anything else?
9. Should we want to please God more than anything else?
10. Would we want to do what God tells us so He will be pleased with us?

You can find this story in your Bible in Matthew 13:46.

31. Jesus Has No Place to Stay

Where do you live? Do you live in a house or an apartment? Most people have a place to live. Even the animals have places they can live and rest.

One day when Jesus was walking along, a man came to Him and told Jesus he wanted to stay with Him and live with Him all the time. But Jesus told the man that He had no home to live in.

Jesus said that the little birds had homes, for they had their nests up in the trees. Jesus also said that the foxes had holes in the ground where they could live. All the wild animals had homes, because they could live in caves and holes. But then Jesus said He had no home where He could go when He was tired and wanted to lie down to rest.

This was because Jesus was so poor that He had no home. He did not have a job where He made money so he could live in a house. He was even poorer than the birds and the animals because even they had a place to live.

But Jesus was not always poor. Before he came to be born on earth, Jesus lived in heaven. He was not poor there, because he was God's Son and He had everything.

Why, then, would Jesus leave heaven and come here to live with us where He would be poor and have trouble? It was because He loved us, and He wanted to make us God's children. Then we can go to heaven, too, after we die. We can live with God there, just as Jesus did.

If Jesus loved us so much that He would leave everything in heaven to come to our world for us, we should love Him, too.

1. What did the man who came to Jesus tell him that he wanted to do?
2. What did Jesus say about the birds and animals?
3. Where did Jesus live before coming to earth to be with people like us?
4. Should we love Jesus even more for doing this for all of us?

You can find this story in your Bible in Matthew 8:18-20 and Luke 9:57-58.

32. Jesus in the Storm at Sea

One day Jesus got into a boat with His disciples, His helpers. They were going to sail across a large lake, called a sea. While they were sailing on the water, Jesus lay down with His head on a pillow. He went to sleep in the boat.

Suddenly a big wind came that made the waves on the water very high and rough. The water began to come into the boat and the disciples were afraid the boat might sink.

Have you ever been on a boat on the water when a storm comes? It can be scary if the boat starts to rock back and forth and the water begins to come in the boat. You might be afraid, too, just like the disciples in the boat with Jesus. They still had to go a long way before they would reach the other side of the sea. They thought they might not make it there before the ship sank in the water.

So the disciples saw Jesus still sleeping through the storm and they went to Him and woke Him up. Then they asked Jesus to save them so they would not drown in the stormy sea.

But Jesus asked the disciples why they were afraid of the winds and the sea while He was with them to keep them safe. Jesus stood up in the boat and He told the wind not to blow and He told the waves to be still. Then the wind stopped blowing and the waves became still and smooth.

When the disciples saw this, they were amazed, for it was another miracle. They said to one another, "Even the wind and the sea obey Him."

After this, the boat sailed the rest of the way across the sea. When it came to the other shore, Jesus and the disciples got out of the boat and walked up safely on the land.

1. What did Jesus get into to sail across the sea with His disciples?
2. Where did Jesus lay His head down and go to sleep?
3. What happened after Jesus fell asleep?
4. What did the wind do to the waves?
5. What did the disciples think after the water began coming into the boat?
6. What did the disciples do then?
7. Should they have been afraid while Jesus was with them?
8. What did Jesus say to the wind and the waves?
9. Did the wind and the waves obey Jesus?

You can find this story in your Bible in Matthew 8:23-27; Mark 4:35-41; and Luke 8:22-25.

33. Jesus Heals a Man with Evil Spirits

You know about the good angels that live in heaven. They they are spirits. But there are some bad spirits, too. They do not live in heaven, because no one who is bad or wicked can live there. These bad spirits are also called evil spirits.

These evil spirits are not like us. They do not have hands and feet and bodies like ours. We cannot see them. They can go into places where we cannot go. Sometimes they go into men and women, and even into children. In Jesus' time, some people had evil spirits living in them.

When Jesus got out of the boat after He had made the wind stop blowing and the waves calm, He met a man who had evil spirits in him. The evil spirits made the man very angry and mean, so that he was almost like a wild animal. All the people were afraid to go near this man.

The man's friends had tried to keep him at home. They even put chains on his hands and feet to keep him there. But the evil spirits were so mean that the man broke the chains. He left his house to go out and live in the mountains.

There were many caves in these mountains. Caves are hollow places in the ground. Some had been dug out of the mountains to bury people who died. This man with the evil spirits used to go live in the caves.

At night the man did not sleep. All night he cried out with a loud voice. Sometimes he would pick up sharp stones from the ground and cut himself. The evil spirits made him do all these things.

The poor man could not make the evil spirits leave him alone. But Jesus had done many miracles, and He could make the evil spirits come out of the man. So when Jesus met the man and saw how he was, He spoke to the evil spirits and told them to come out of the man.

At once, the evil spirits left the man. But they needed another place to go. There were a lot of pigs nearby, eating the grass that grew on the mountainside. So when the evil spirits left the

nan, they went into the pigs. Then the pigs ran
own the hill into the sea.

But the man was not angry and mean any-
nore! He was suddenly quiet and well, like other
eople. Jesus had made the evil spirits go away.
o the man thanked Jesus. He wanted to go with
esus and stay with Him all the time. But Jesus
old him to go back to his home and tell his
riends how he had been made well.

. Where do angels live?
. Where do the evil spirits go sometimes?
. Who met Jesus when He came out of the boat
   after crossing the sea?

You can find this story in your Bible in Mark 5:1-
0 and Luke 8:26-39

34. Jesus Cures a Woman Who Touches Him

Jesus and His disciples went again to the city called Capernaum. A great crowd of people followed Him. Some of these people were pushing and pressing against Jesus.

In the crowd was a woman who had been sick for a very long time, for twelve years. She had asked a lot of doctors to make her well. She had given them all her money, so now she was poor. But not one of the doctors could cure her. Now she was in the crowd that was following Jesus.

Perhaps the woman had heard how Jesus had healed many people. Many had heard of Jesus' miracles and had come to find him. The woman believed that Jesus could help her. So she was following Him to try to get close to Jesus. As soon as she saw Him she said to herself, If I can only come behind Him and touch His clothes, I am sure I will be well.

So the woman came up softly behind Jesus and put out her hand and touched the robe He was wearing. At once she felt that she was well.

When this happened, Jesus stopped and looked around. He asked who had touched Him. The disciples had not seen the woman do it, and they wondered how Jesus could ask who had touched Him. There were so many people pressing against Him in the crowd, it could have been anyone. But Jesus said someone had touched Him and been made well.

When the poor woman saw that Jesus knew someone had touched Him and that she could not hide herself from Him, she was afraid. She came trembling to Jesus and kneeled down on the ground in front of Him. Then she told Jesus what she had done and how in a minute she was cured of her sickness.

Jesus spoke kindly to her and called her Daughter. He said she did right when she came to Him to be made well. And then Jesus told her to go to her home and not be afraid anymore. He was glad that she believed that Jesus could heal her.

1. When Jesus came to the city, who was in the crowd that followed him?
2. How long had the woman been sick?
3. Had any of the doctors made her well?
4. What did she say to herself when she saw Jesus?
5. What happened after she touched Jesus' robe?
6. Did Jesus know someone had touched Him?
7. When the woman saw that she could not hide from Jesus, what did she do?
8. What did Jesus call her?
9. Did Jesus tell the woman not to be afraid anymore?

You can find this story in your Bible in Matthew 9:20-22: Mark 5:25-34; and Luke 8:43-48.

35. Jesus Heals a Little Girl

While Jesus was speaking to some people, a man came to Him. This man was in great trouble because his little girl was sick. He was afraid she might die. So he went to find Jesus to see if He could help his daughter. When he found Jesus, he begged Him to come to his house and put His hands on his little girl and make her well.

So Jesus left with the man to go to his house. When they got near the house, somebody came out and told them it was too late. He said the little girl was dead and it was not worthwhile for Jesus to come any further. But Jesus told the man not to be troubled, because his daughter would be alive again.

When Jesus went into the man's house, the people were all crying, because they were so sorry that the little girl was dead. Then Jesus told all the people to leave. He took three of His disciples and the little girl's father and mother and went into the girl's room where she lay.

Jesus walked over to her bed and took hold of her hand. Then He said to the girl, "Arise." As soon as Jesus said this, the little girl became alive again. She got up from her bed and walked. She was only twelve years old.

Then Jesus told the people to give her something to eat, for she must be very hungry. Her mother and father were very happy because their little daughter was alive again. Now they would have her to live with them and she could grow up with her family. And she would love them as she used to before she died.

1. When the man came to find Jesus, why was he in great trouble?
2. Who in the man's family was very sick?
3. What did he ask Jesus to do?
4. Did Jesus go to the man's house?
5. What happened when they got near the house?
6. Did Jesus go to the house anyway?
7. When they went into the house, what were the people doing?
8. When Jesus went into the little girl's room, what did He do?
9. What happened to the little girl then?
10. How did her mother and father feel when they saw she was   alive again?

You can find this story in your Bible in Matthew 9:18-19,23-26; Mark 5:21-24,35-43; and Luke 8:40-42,49-56.

36. Jesus Heals the Blind and Dumb

As Jesus left that place, two blind men followed Him. They could not see Him, but someone had told them that Jesus was there. Perhaps they had heard how Jesus had brought the little girl to life again, and they thought He could make them see again.

So the blind men followed Jesus and called after Him. They begged Jesus to heal them, to help them see again. Jesus stopped and asked the two men if they thought He was able to make them see. They said, "Yes, Lord."

Then Jesus said He would do it. He put out His hand and touched their eyes and they were well. By only touching them, Jesus made them see again.

Then the men went away and told all the people who lived in that country how Jesus had healed them in one moment. He had made them able to see.

After they heard how Jesus had healed the blind men, some people brought another man to Jesus. He was dumb, or mute. He could not speak. Once he had been able to speak like you and me, but now an evil spirit had gone into him. The evil spirit would not allow him to speak.

None of the man's friends could make the evil spirit go out. So they brought their friend to Jesus so He could make the evil spirit leave. Then Jesus made the evil spirit go out and the man was able to speak again.

The people who watched Jesus heal this man said they had never seen such a wonderful miracle before.

1. What was wrong with the two men who followed Jesus?
2. What did the blind men want Jesus to do?
3. Did Jesus ask the men if they thought He could heal them?
4. How did Jesus make their eyes well?
5. What did the blind men do after they were made well?

6. When the people heard about it, who did they bring to Jesus?
7. What made the man unable to speak?
8. Could the man's friends make the evil spirit go out of the man?
9. What did Jesus do?
10. Was the man able to speak after that?

You can find this story in your Bible in Matthew 9:27-33 and Luke 11:14.

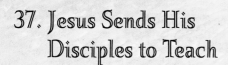

37. Jesus Sends His Disciples to Teach

After this, Jesus visited many other cities to teach the people who lived there. Wherever He went, He talked to crowds of people and He healed many people. His disciples also went with Him. They listened to His teachings and they watched as He made many people well.

But soon Jesus knew He could not teach all the people in the country by Himself. There were too many of them. So Jesus decided to send out His twelve disciples to teach the people who lived in the cities where Jesus would not be able to go.

By this time the disciples had been with Jesus for a while. They knew what He wanted to teach the people He met. They knew Jesus had come from heaven to save the people from their sins. They knew Jesus was God's Son.

Before Jesus sent the disciples out He gave them some advice. He told them to take nothing with them. He said the people they met would take care of them. And He told them that if people did not listen to what they taught about Jesus, then they should leave and go to the next town.

So the twelve disciples went out to other cities. They went out in pairs, or two by two. They taught people about Jesus. They told them how God had sent Jesus from heaven to come and live with them and show them how to be God's children. Jesus also let the disciples make sick people well and dead people alive, just as Jesus did Himself. Jesus let them do these wonderful things so that the people would listen to what they said and believe that God had sent them.

After the disciples had traveled to other cities and taught many people about Jesus, they returned to Jesus. They told Him where they had been and what they had done.

1. Why could Jesus not teach all the people in that land by Himself?
2. Who did He send to teach the people in the cities where He could not go?
3. What did Jesus tell the disciples before they left?
4. What did He allow the disciples to do while they were teaching the people in the cities where they went?
5. What did the disciples teach the people about Jesus?
6. Where did the disciples go after they went to the cities to teach the people?

You can find this story in your Bible in Matthew 10:1,7-14; Mark 6:6-13; and Luke 9:1-6.

38. Jesus Feeds a Great Crowd

Then Jesus and his disciples got into a boat and sailed to another place across the sea. They wanted to be alone. But when the people saw Jesus going across the water, they followed after Him. Soon a great crowd of men and women and children came to the place where Jesus was.

Even though Jesus had wanted to be alone, He was very kind to the people. He taught them many things about God and about heaven. He even healed many people who were sick.

When it began to get dark, the disciples asked Jesus to send the people away. It was time to eat but the people did not have any food. Jesus said the disciples should give the people something to eat.

The disciples asked, "Where shall we get food for so many? Shall we go out and buy two hundred pennies worth of bread for them? That would not be enough to give each one even a little."

Then Jesus asked the disciples how many loaves of bread they had. They said they had only five loaves of bread and two small fish. This was what a young boy had.

Then Jesus told the disciples to tell all the people to sit down in rows on the grass. There were thousands of people. Jesus took the loaves of bread and the fish and held them in His hand. He looked up into the sky and thanked God for them. Then Jesus broke the bread and the fish into pieces and gave the pieces to the disciples. The disciples took the pieces and passed them out to the people.

As soon as they gave a piece of bread or fish to a person, another piece came. And when they gave that piece, another piece came. And so the pieces of bread and fish kept on coming until all the men, women and little children had as much as they wanted to eat.

After all the people had eaten, Jesus told the disciples to pick up the pieces of food left on the ground. The disciples picked up twelve baskets full of pieces. This was a lot more than they had when they first began to feed the people.

This was a miracle. Jesus could do miracles because He is the Son of God and He can do the same things God can do.

1. Who followed Jesus and His disciples across the sea?
2. Did the disciples have enough food or money to feed all the people?
3. What did Jesus do with the loaves and fish when He took them in His hand?

You can find this story in your Bible in Matthew 14:13-21; Mark 6:32-44; Luke 9:10-17; and John 6:1-15.

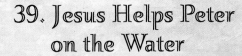

39. Jesus Helps Peter on the Water

After all the people had eaten as much as they wanted and the disciples collected the food left over, Jesus sent the people back to their homes. He sent the disciples away in a boat to sail back to the other side of the big lake. But Jesus stayed by Himself on the shore.

When the disciples had gone, Jesus went up onto a mountain alone. He kneeled down on the ground and prayed to God.

Later, Jesus came down from the mountain and stood on the shore. He saw the disciples who were still in the middle of the sea. They were rowing their boat, trying to get to the other side. But the wind was blowing the wrong way and the waves were rough and stormy.

Then Jesus went out to the boat, walking on top of the water. When the disciples looked up and saw Jesus coming, they were afraid. They cried out because they were afraid it was a spirit coming toward them.

But Jesus said to them, "Do not be afraid. It is I."

One of the disciples, Peter, spoke to Jesus from the boat. He asked Jesus if he could come to Him on the water. And Jesus told Peter to come.

Then Peter got down out of the boat and began to walk on the water to Jesus.

But when Peter heard the loud winds and felt the waves crashing around him, he was afraid. He began to sink in the water. Then He cried out to Jesus, "Lord, save me, or I will drown."

Jesus put out His hand and held Peter up so that he did not sink down under the water. Then He asked Peter why he was afraid while he was with Him. As long as Jesus was with Peter, He would take care of him and save him from being hurt.

Then Jesus and Peter came into the boat. They traveled the rest of the way across the sea to the place where they wanted to land. When they got out of the boat and walked on the land, people heard that Jesus was there. Then they began to bring their sick friends to Jesus for Him to make them all well.

Wherever Jesus went, the people brought sick friends and family lying on beds and laid them in the streets, so that they might even touch Jesus' clothes as He passed by. And everyone who touched Jesus was made well.

1. Why were the disciples afraid when they saw Jesus?
2. What did Peter do?
3. What happened to Peter while He was walking to Jesus?

You can find this story in your Bible in Matthew 14:22-33; Mark 6:45-51; and John 6:15-21.

40. Jesus Heals a Woman's Daughter

One day a woman came to Jesus and told Him that an evil spirit had gone into her daughter. She said the spirit troubled her daughter. The woman begged Jesus to make the spirit leave her daughter and go away.

At first Jesus turned away from the woman, as if He would not listen to her. He did this only to find out whether or not the woman really believed Jesus could cure her child. Many people who came to Jesus really believed He could heal people, but others did not believe.

When the woman saw Jesus turn away, she did not stop praying to Him. Instead, she only prayed to Him more. She kneeled down at His feet and said, "Lord, help me."

Then Jesus told the woman that because she believed He could make her daughter well, and because she kept praying to Him, He would do it. He said He would heal her daughter from the evil spirit.

When the woman went back to her house, she looked for her daughter. Then she found out that the evil spirit had gone out and her daughter was well. She was very happy because Jesus had healed her daughter.

Jesus did another miracle. Not only did He heal the woman's daughter from the evil spirit, He did it without even being near her daughter. Many times Jesus was able to heal someone without even being with them. He could do this because He is God's Son. Jesus can do anything God can do. And God loves all people and wants to help them.

1. What did the woman come to tell Jesus?
2. What was wrong with the woman's daughter?
3. Did Jesus answer the woman at first?
4. What did He do?
5. Why did He turn away from the woman?
6. Did the woman go away, or keep praying to Jesus?

7. When Jesus saw this, what did He say He would do for the woman?
8. What did the woman find when she got home?
9. Did Jesus have to be near someone to heal them?

You can find this story in your Bible in Matthew 15:21-28 and Mark 7:24-30.

41. Jesus Helps a Blind Man See

Jesus came to a city called Bethsaida. While He was there some people brought a man to Him. The man was blind. He could not see anything. That is why the people had to take him to Jesus. He could not find Jesus on his own.

This man had friends who felt sorry for him. They wanted him to be able to see again, for they knew his life was hard because he was blind.

When the men brought the blind man to Jesus, they did so because they believed Jesus could help him. They had heard how Jesus had healed many other people, including those who were blind. So they begged Jesus to make the blind man able to see again.

When Jesus had heard the men asking for His help, He loved the man and wanted to heal him.

So He took the blind man by the hand and led him out of town.

Then Jesus put His hands on the blind man's eyes. He asked the man if he could see.

The blind man said, yes, he could see, but he could not see very well. As the man looked up he said that he could tell people were passing by, but they did not look like men. They looked so large and high that they seemed to be trees walking along.

So Jesus put His hands on the blind man's eyes again. The man looked up again, and looked all around. This time he could see everything clearly. He knew then that Jesus had healed him. He had been blind, but now he could see.

After this, Jesus told the man to go straight to his home. He told the man not to tell anyone in the town what had happened. At that time, many people were not happy with how many people were following Jesus, and some people even wanted to hurt Jesus. So He told the man to go home and not say anything about what had happened.

1. When Jesus came to the town of Bethsaida, who did some men bring to Him?
2. What did they want Jesus to do for this blind man?
3. What did Jesus do to the blind man's eyes to make them well?
4. What did the man say that people passing by looked like?
5. What did Jesus do to the man's eyes a second time?
6. Was the man able to see everything clearly after that?
7. What did Jesus tell the man to do after He had made him see again?

You can find this story in your Bible in Mark 8:22-26.

42. Jesus on the Mountain

After a while, Jesus took three of His disciples with Him and went up on a mountain to pray. The disciples were Peter, James, and John.

While Jesus was praying, His face began to change. It became very bright and shining, like the sun in the sky. And His clothes changed, too. They began to look as white as new snow.

Suddenly, two more men appeared with Jesus. They did not look like other men. They looked more beautiful. It was because these two men, named Moses and Elijah, had come from the place where people who love God go when they die.

We do not know where that place is. But these two men lived there. Now they had come back to this world where we live and where they used to live. But they had only come back for a little while to talk with Jesus.

Now the three disciples had been asleep and they suddenly woke up. When they did, they saw how Jesus' face and clothes were bright as the sun. And they saw the two men with Jesus. Peter wanted to build shelters on the mountain for Jesus and Moses and Elijah.

But then a bright cloud came on the mountain. It covered Peter, James, and John. They heard a voice speaking out of the cloud. It was God's voice. It said that Jesus was God's dear Son, and that the disciples should obey Jesus.

When the disciples heard God's voice, they were very much afraid. They kneeled down and put their faces to the ground. But Jesus came to them and put His hand on them. Then He told them to stand up and not be afraid.

As the disciples stood up, they looked around. The two men were not there now. They had gone back to the other world where they lived.

Then Jesus and the three disciples went back down the mountain. And Jesus told the disciples not to tell anyone what they had seen on the mountain.

1. Who did Jesus take with Him when He went up on the mountain to pray?
2. While Jesus was praying, what happened to His face?
3. Who suddenly appeared and talked to Jesus?
4. Did they look different from other men?
5. What came on the mountain and covered the disciples?
6. What did they hear coming out of the cloud?
7. What did God's voice say to the disciples?

You can find this story in your Bible in Matthew 17:1-9; Mark 9:2-10; and Luke 9:28-36.

43. Jesus Heals a Man's Son

After Jesus and the disciples came down from the mountain, a crowd gathered around them. Out of the crowd came a man. He went to Jesus and kneeled down on the ground in front of Him.

Then the man said, "Master, I have brought my son to you because an evil spirit has gone into him. Sometimes this evil spirit makes my son fall into the fire, and sometimes into the water, because it wants to kill him."

Then Jesus said, "Bring your son to me."

So they brought the boy to Jesus. While they were bringing him, the evil spirit made him fall down on the ground. Then Jesus asked the boy's father how long ago it was when the evil spirit first went into his son.

The boy's father said it was many years ago, when the boy was a little child. And the man said to Jesus, "If you can do anything for us, please help us."

Then Jesus said to the evil spirit, "Come out of the young man, and do not go into him again."

Then the evil spirit came out of the man's son. But as the spirit was coming out, it shook the young man and made him so week and sick it seemed as if he were dead. In fact, many of the people who saw him lying on the ground said, "He is dead."

But Jesus took the young man by the hand and picked him up off the ground. And the young man stood on his feet and was well.

Then Jesus gave him back to his father.

1. What was wrong with the young man who was brought to Jesus?
2. Where did the evil spirit make him fall sometimes?
3. Why did the evil spirit do this?
4. How long had the evil spirit been in the man's son?
5. What did Jesus say to the evil spirit?

6. Did the spirit obey Jesus?
7. What did the spirit do to the young man as it was coming out?
8. What did many of the people say as they saw the young man lying on the ground?
9. But when Jesus took him by the hand and lifted him up, was he well?

You can find this story in your Bible in Matthew 17:14-21; Mark 9:14-29; and Luke 9:37-43.

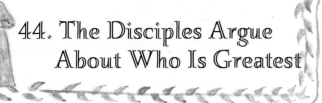

44. The Disciples Argue About Who Is Greatest

One day the disciples were walking along together toward Capernaum. As they walked, they began to argue with each other. Each one of them said that all the rest ought to listen to him. Each one said he was greater than the others. And this made them argue.

When they came into the house where they were staying, Jesus asked them what they had been talking about. But they were ashamed and did not want to tell Him. They did not know He had heard them arguing as they walked along, but He had. So they were ashamed.

Jesus knows everything we say and He knew what the disciples said as they walked along. He did not want them each thinking they were better or greater than the others.

So Jesus told the disciples that they must not want other people to listen to them and mind them, but they must listen to others and mind what they say. God loves every person the same and does not want people to think too much of themselves.

Jesus also is not pleased with us when we are too proud and when we think of ourselves as better than others. He is pleased with us when we think of others before ourselves.

Jesus wanted his disciples to understand what He had come to teach people. He wanted them to begin to show people how God wanted people to live. He knew they could not show people how to please God if they were arguing with each other.

Jesus knew that even though He had been kind to people in that country, some people did not love Him. Why did they not love Jesus? Because He told them about the things they did that were wrong, their sins. Their sins were the bad things they did, and Jesus told them they must stop doing those things to please God.

But the people did not want to stop. They were selfish. They did not want to be told about their sins and that God would punish them for their sins if they did not stop doing the wrong things. The people wanted to live their lives without thinking about what God wanted them to do.

Since Jesus was telling the people about their sins, they were angry with Jesus for telling them. They wanted Jesus to go away. They even talked about trying to kill Jesus so that He could not speak to them about their sins anymore.

But Jesus knew what people were going to do to Him. He told the disciples that someday the people would kill Him. But He also told them He would come back to life again. He would come out of the grave where people would bury Him.

His disciples did not really understand. But Jesus knew that they would one day. And He knew He would need His disciples to tell others about Him. So He wanted them to begin to live in ways that would please God.

That is why Jesus did not want the disciples to argue with each other. He wanted them to show people how we are to love each other like God wants us to.

1. What did the disciples do as they were walking along toward Capernaum?
2. What were they arguing about?
3. Did they think Jesus had heard what they said?
4. Does Jesus know everything we say?
5. When Jesus asked the disciples why they were arguing, how did they feel?
6. Did He say that they should think they are better than other people?
7. Is Jesus pleased when we are too proud, or when we think we are better than other people?

You can find this story in your Bible in Matthew 18:1; Mark 9:33-35; and Luke 9:46.

45. Peter Finds Money in a Fish's Mouth

In the city of Jerusalem was a beautiful church called the Temple. There were men who worked in the Temple. They helped keep up the Temple and do the things God wanted done in the Temple where people came learn about Him. These men in the Temple were called priests. They were like the ministers or pastors in your church.

These priests did not have other jobs. The people in the city who went to the Temple sent money to the priests so they could buy food and have a place to live.

One day a man came to the disciple named Peter. He asked Peter for some money to send to the priests at the Temple. The man thought Jesus and the disciples should be paying some money to help the priests, too.

Peter went to Jesus and asked Him about it. Jesus told Peter He would give the man some money for the Temple priests.

But Jesus was poor. Where would He get the money? This is how Jesus told Peter to get the money. He said Peter should take a long line, or string, and put a sharp hook on the end of it. Then he should let the hook down into the water in the lake while holding onto the string.

Jesus said that a fish would come and be caught on the hook. Then Peter must pull up the fish out of the water and open its mouth. There in the fish's mouth he would find a piece of money.

So Peter did as Jesus told him. He took a line of string and tied a sharp hook to the end of it. Then he went to the lake and let the hook down into the water. A fish did come along and was caught on the hook.

When Peter felt the fish pulling at the line and trying to get away, he pulled up the line and yanked it out of the water. The fish was caught onto the hook. Peter took the hook into his hand and opened its mouth. There, inside the fish's mouth, was a piece of money, just as Jesus had said.

Then Peter gave the money to the man who had asked him for it, so he could send it to the priests at the Temple.

1. What did the people of Jerusalem send the ministers at the Temple?
2. When a man came to ask Peter for some money to send to the priests, did Jesus say He would give the man some money?
3. Where did Jesus tell Peter to find the money?

You can find this story in your Bible in Matthew 17:24-27.

46. Jesus Tells About a King's Servant

Jesus told his disciples a story about a king. This king had a servant who worked for him. The servant had some of the king's money. Now the king wanted him to pay it back.

But the servant could not do this. It was a lot of money, and the man had no money to pay the king with. Then the king said that the servant and the servant's wife and all his little children must be sold, so that the king might get the money that was paid for them. He wanted to do this because the servant could not pay him.

But when the servant heard what the king said, he was very sorry. He went to see the king and kneeled down on the ground before him. Then he begged the king to wait a little while until he could go and try to get some money.

Then, as soon as he got the money, he said, he would come back and pay the king all that he owed him.

When the king saw how upset the servant was, he felt sorry for the servant. Then he said that the servant and his wife and their little children should not be sold. Then he told the servant that he would forget about the money he owed him and that the servant would never have to pay it back.

Then the servant was very glad and he thanked the king for being so kind to him.

But when the servant left the king's house, he met a man he knew who owed him some money. The servant told the man that he must pay him back the money he owned him. But the man said he could not do it. He said he would pay it as soon as he could, but he could not do it right then.

But the king's servant would not wait. He grabbed the man and said, "Pay me what you owe me."

Because the poor man could not do this a

nce, the servant had him sent to prison, to be shut up there until he got his money back.

When the king heard what his servant had done to the man, he was very angry. After all, he had forgotten about the money his servant owed him. And now the servant would not forget about money someone else owed him. Yet it was not nearly as much money as the servant had owed the king.

The king called the servant to him and said, "O wicked servant. I forgave you when you could not pay me, and you ought to forgive this poor man when he cannot pay you."

Then the king sent the mean servant away to prison to be punished.

Jesus told this story to teach us that we must be willing to forgive other people when they have done wrong to us, or when they owe us something they cannot pay. If we do not forgive other people, God will not forgive us when we do wrong.

1. What did the servant owe the king?
2. When the servant could not pay what he owed the king, what did the king say should be to him, his wife, and his children?
3. When the servant heard this, what did he kneel down and ask the king to do?
4. Who did the servant meet when he left the king's house?
5. When the man asked the servant for more time to pay back the money, what did the servant say to him?
6. Where did he send the man?
7. How did the king feel when he heard what the servant did?

You can find this story in your Bible in Matthew 18:23-35.

47. Jesus Stops James and John from Being Angry

While Jesus and His disciples were walking along together, they came near a little town, or village. A lot of people lived in this village. Jesus thought they might be able to go into the village and rest and eat. He and his disciples had been walking for a while and they were tired and hungry.

So Jesus sent some of the disciples into the village to ask the people there if they could stop in the village and rest, and get some food to eat.

But the people in the village were unkind to Jesus. They would not let Him stop in their town to rest, or give Him any food to eat. When the disciples heard this, two of them got very angry. Their names were James and John. They were so angry at the whole village that they wanted to punish the people for being unkind to Jesus.

James and John were so angry, they asked Jesus to let them bring fire down from the sky. Then the fire would burn up the houses in the village and all the people who lived there.

But Jesus would not let them do this. He was not pleased with James and John for wanting to do so cruel a thing. Jesus told them that He did not come down to this world to kill people. He came to save them from dying.

Jesus said He would not punish the people who were unkind to Him. Instead, He went on to another village and stopped there to rest and get food to eat.

We might get angry at people sometimes. Some people are not kind to us, and we do not know why. That might make us angry. Some people might take things that belong to us, or make fun of us. That could make us angry, too.

But Jesus tells us we must not let our anger make us want to hurt others. Instead of letting His disciples hurt the people in the village, He went on to another town. Sometimes instead of getting angry at people who are not kind to us, we should just leave them alone. That is what Jesus would tell us to do.

1. Why did Jesus and the disciples need a place to rest and get something to eat?
2. What did the people in the village say to the disciples when they asked if they could rest and eat in the village?
3. How did James and John feel when the people said this?
4. What did they ask Jesus to let them do to punish the people?
5. What did Jesus say to James and John for wanting to do such a cruel thing?

You can find this story in your Bible in Luke 9:52-56.

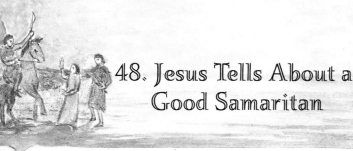

48. Jesus Tells About a Good Samaritan

Jesus told the people another story about a man who was walking along a lonely road. There were rocks and caves beside this road, where robbers used to hide. Suddenly, some robbers came out of hiding and stopped the man and took away his money, his clothes, and everything he had.

They also beat the man and hurt him so much he could not walk any further. Then the robbers went away and left him lying there, almost dead.

After a while a man came to the place where the man was lying in the road. This man was a priest who stayed at the Temple and taught the people to be good and kind to each other.

But he was not good and kind himself. He would not help the poor, hurt man. Instead, he crossed over to the other side of the road and pretended he did not see the man.

Soon another man passed by. But he did not help the poor man, either. He walked on by, just as the priest had done.

After these two selfish men had gone by, along came a third man. He was riding on a donkey. This man was a Samaritan. Samaritans lived in a country called Samaria. Some people did not like Samaritans. In fact, sometimes people would not even talk to them.

Most people would not expect a Samaritan to stop and help someone who was hurt. But this man stopped as soon as he saw the man lying on the road.

He lifted up the man very carefully and put him on the donkey. He took him to a house nearby and stayed with the man all night and took care of his wounds.

The next day, the Samaritan gave some money to the man who lived in the house and asked him to take care of the sick man.

Jesus told this story to teach us that we must be like the Good Samaritan. We must be kind to people who are poor and sick. Whenever we can, we must help others who need help.

Jesus said that everyone deserves to be helped, because God loves us all.

1. Who came out of the rocks by the road and stopped the man as he traveled?
2. When the Samaritan came by, what did he do for the man in the road?
3. What are we supposed to learn from this story Jesus told?

You can find this story in your Bible in Luke 10:30-37.

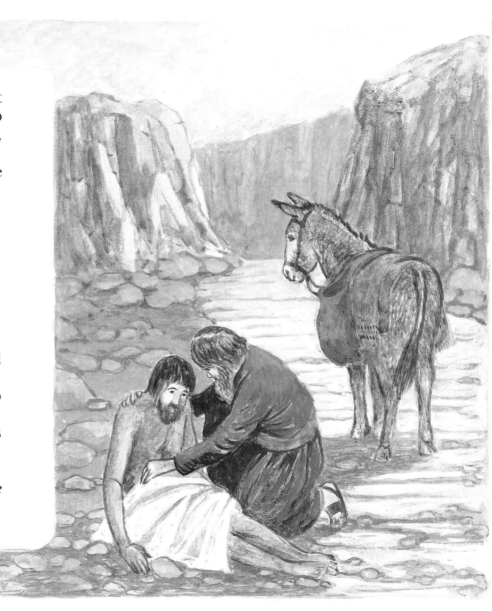

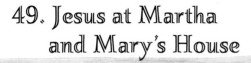

49. Jesus at Martha and Mary's House

One day Jesus came to a village called Bethany. A woman named Martha lived there with her sister, Mary. She asked Jesus to come to her house.

When Jesus came into the house, Mary stopped doing her work. She wanted to hear what Jesus had to say, so she sat down by His feet to listen to His teaching. Mary wanted Jesus to teach her how her sins might be taken away, so she could know how to please God. She knew Jesus could tell her how to live that way.

But Martha was not sitting with Jesus. She was working in the kitchen. Martha thought that Mary should keep on doing her work. So she went into the room and asked Jesus to tell Mary to go back to her work, to help Martha.

But Jesus said that Mary was doing the right thing by stopping her work to listen to Him. It was better for Mary to learn about the things He taught, Jesus told Martha, than to go on doing her work around the house.

He told Martha she was worried about the wrong things by being so upset about Mary not working. Jesus said listening to His teaching was more important.

1. What was the name of the woman who asked Jesus to come to her house?
2. What was the name of Martha's sister?
3. When Jesus came into the house, what did Mary do?
4. Where was Martha?
5. Why did Mary sit at Jesus' feet?
6. Was Martha happy about this?
7. What did she think Mary should be doing?
8. What did Martha ask Jesus to do?
9. Did Jesus tell Mary to go back to her work?
10. Why did Jesus tell Martha that Mary was doing the right thing?

You can find this story in your Bible in Luke 10:38-42.

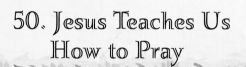

50. Jesus Teaches Us How to Pray

Jesus spent a lot of time by himself praying to God. One day the disciples saw Jesus praying alone. When He was finished, one of the disciples said to Him, "Lord, teach us to pray."

So Jesus taught His disciples how to pray to God.

He said, "When you pray, say,

Our Father, who art in Heaven,
Hallowed be Thy name.
Thy Kingdom come, Thy will be done
  On earth as it is in heaven.
Give us this day our daily bread.
And forgive us our debts,
  As we forgive our debtors.
And lead us not into temptation,
  But deliver us from evil.

For Thine is the kingdom
  and the power and the glory,
  forever.

Amen."

This is called the Lord's Prayer because the Lord Jesus taught it to us. You might have heard it in your church. But it might be hard to understand.

"Our Father who art in heaven," means that we pray to God, who we call our Father who lives in heaven.

"Hallowed be Thy name," means God is holy and perfect. When we pray we should say that we know He is holy and good.

"Thy kingdom come," means we want God's way of living life to come to earth so we can be happy and live to please God.

"Thy will be done on earth as it is in heaven," means we want life on earth to be like it is in heaven, where everything is perfect and happy with God.

"Give us this day our daily bread," means we

ask God to give us what we need each day, like food and clothes.

"And forgive us our debts as we forgive our debtors," means we ask God to forgive and forget our sins just like we forgive and forget the wrong things that people do to us.

"And lead us not into temptation, but deliver us from evil," means we ask God to help us when we want to do something wrong, and we ask Him to keep bad things away from us.

"For Thine is the kingdom and the power and the glory, forever," means that God made everything and everything belongs to Him. It also means that God can do anything.

We must remember that when we pray this prayer or other prayers, we are talking to God. We must think about what we are saying to God.

Jesus not only teaches us to say the Lord's Prayer, but He tells us to pray to God for everything that we need. God is our Father who lives in heaven, and He loves to give His children the things they pray to Him for.

1. What was Jesus doing when the disciples saw Him?
2. What did the disciples ask Jesus to do?
3. What is the name of the prayer that Jesus taught them?
4. When we say this prayer, who are we speaking to?
5. What does "Hallowed be Thy name" mean?
6. What does it mean to ask God to "give us our daily bread"?
7. Does Jesus tell us to pray to God for everything we need?
8. Does God love to give His children the things they ask Him for?

You can find this story in your Bible in Matthew 6:9-13 and Luke 11:1-4.

51. Jesus Uses Mud to Heal a Man's Sight

As Jesus was walking along the street, He saw a man who was blind. This man had always been blind. He had not been able to see since he was born. Now that he had grown up, he could not work and earn money because he was blind.

So the blind man sat down in the street, and begged the people who passed by to give him some of their money. He asked for it because he could not work and he needed money to buy food to eat and clothes to wear.

When the disciples saw the man, they asked Jesus what the man had done wrong to make him blind since birth. But Jesus said the man had not done anything wrong.

When Jesus saw the man, He was sorry for him. So He stooped down and took some mud from the ground and put it on the blind man's eyes. Then He told him to go out and wash off his eyes in a pool of water called the Pool of Siloam.

Then the man went to the pool and washed the mud off his eyes. After he did, he found that he could see. But it was not the mud or the water that made him see. It was Jesus who cured him and gave him back his sight.

The people who had known the blind man saw him walking along like any other person, with no one to lead him. They wondered what happened. They said, "Is this the man who used to sit in the street and beg?"

Some of them said, "Yes, this is the man."

Other people said, "This is not the blind man. It is another man who looks like him."

But the man himself said, "I am the one you are talking about."

Then the people asked him how he had been made well and he told them how Jesus had healed him.

But the men who asked him were not happy when he said this, because these men were wicked. They were some of the men who did not love Jesus and did not believe He could make blind men see. So when the man said it was Jesus who healed him, these men would not speak to him or have anything to do with him anymore.

When Jesus heard how they were treating the man, He went to find him. He told him that it was God's Son who made him well. Before that, the man did not know that Jesus was God's Son. When the man heard this, he kneeled down on the ground and worshiped Jesus.

1. What was wrong with the man who Jesus saw begging in the street?
2. Why was the blind man begging and asking people for money?
3. What did the disciples ask Jesus about the man?
4. Did Jesus say the blind man had done anything wrong to be blind?
5. What did Jesus put on the blind man's eyes?
6. When the man went to the pool to wash his eyes, what happened?
7. Had the water or mud cured him, or did Jesus heal his eyes?
8. How did the people treat the man when he told them it was Jesus who healed him?
9. When Jesus told the man it was God's Son who made him well, what did the man do?

You can find this story in your Bible in John 9:1-41.

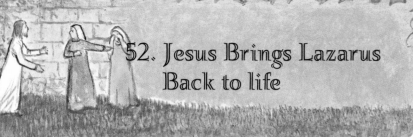

52. Jesus Brings Lazarus Back to life

Remember the story about Jesus' visit to Martha and Mary's house? Jesus went to visit them in their home. They were His friends. Martha and Mary also had a brother named Lazarus.

After Jesus went away from their house the first time, Lazarus got sick. So Martha and Mary sent a message to Jesus that their brother Lazarus was very sick. When Jesus heard this, He was sad and headed back to their house. They were His friends, and Jesus loved Martha, Mary, and Lazarus. But when Jesus got to their house, Lazarus had died. They had already buried him in his grave. The people who were with Martha and Mary were crying, because they were sorry that Lazarus was dead.

Jesus asked them where they had buried Lazarus, and they took Jesus there. This grave was a cave in the side of a hill, with a big stone rolled over the opening to shut it up. Jesus said to the people, "Take away the stone."

So they took the stone away from the door of the cave.

Then Jesus said with a loud voice, "Lazarus, come out!"

As soon as Jesus said this, Lazarus came out of the cave alive. He had cloth wrapped around him, something people in those days did when they buried those who had died.

Jesus had made Lazarus come back alive just by speaking the words. And Jesus told the people to loosen the cloth wrapped around him so Lazarus could walk. Then Lazarus, after he came back to life, went with Martha and Mary to their home again. And he lived with them as he had before.

1. What was the name of Martha and Mary's brother?
2. When Lazarus got sick, whom did Martha and Mary send a message to?
3. What did Jesus do?
4. When Jesus got to Martha and Mary's house, what had happened?
5. Where was Lazarus buried?
6. What was in front of the cave?
7. When they took Jesus to the cave, what did He say after they took the stone away?
8. What happened then?
9. Who made Lazarus become alive again?
10. Was this a miracle?
11. Who can do miracles?
12. After Jesus brought him back to life, where did Lazarus go to live?

You can find this story in your Bible in John 11:1-44.

53. Jesus Heals a Woman on the Sabbath

People in Jesus' country went to church on the Sabbath Day. This is like our Sunday when we go to church. Jesus went into a church on one Sabbath Day. A women was there who had been sick for many years. Her sickness made her bend over, so that she could not stand up straight, as you can.

She bent over when she walked and while she sat. She was bent over all the time. She could not help it.

When Jesus saw the woman, He called her over to Him and told her that she should be well. Then He put His hands on her and suddenly she was healed of her sickness. She could stand up straight like other people. Then she was very happy, because she had not been able to stand up straight for many years. She thanked God for being made well.

There were other people in the church who saw Jesus heal this woman. One man who saw this was angry. He said Jesus should not have cured a sick person on a Sabbath Day. Remember that back then, they had a rule about not working on the Sabbath Day, because God said they should rest. This man thought that healing the woman was like doing work, and that Jesus had broken a rule.

Jesus asked the man if he gave his cow and donkey water to drink on the Sabbath Day. If he did, the man would have to untie the cow and donkey and lead them out to drink. So if it was right to be kind to a donkey and a cow on the Sabbath Day, was it not also right to make this woman well on the Sabbath Day?

Then all the people who had thought Jesus did wrong were ashamed. They could not answer Jesus. But the rest of the people were glad for all the kind things Jesus had done.

1. What was wrong with the woman who was in the church on the Sabbath Day?
2. What did Jesus do for the woman?
3. After Jesus touched her, could she stand up straight?
4. What was the rule in those days about working on the Sabbath Day?

5. Why was the man in the church angry with Jesus for healing the woman?
6. What did Jesus ask the man if he did for his cow and donkey on the Sabbath Day?
7. If it is right to be kind to animals on the Sabbath Day, is it also right to help people on that day?

You can find this story in your Bible in Luke 13:10-17.

54. Jesus Tells About the Prodigal Son

One day Jesus told a story about a man who had two sons. The younger son came to his father and said that he wanted all the money his father was ever going to give him. So his father gave him all the money he had for him.

Then the younger son took the money and left his father's house. He went to a country that was far away and began to spend all his money. Soon he wasted all of it.

Then the son had to find work so he could eat. He went to work for a man in that country but it was not a good job. He worked in the man's fields, feeding his pigs. But the man did not give the son enough food to eat.

One day, the son was sitting with the pigs and he began to feel sorry that he ever left his father's house. He remembered that he used to have plenty of food to eat, even more than he wanted.

So he thought to himself, I will go back to my father, and tell him how sorry I am that I went away and left him. Then maybe my father will forgive me and let me live at his house again. I will even be willing to be his servant.

So the son started to go back to his father's house. Now his father had been waiting a long time for his son to come home because he loved him and missed him. One day the father was looking down the road and he saw his son coming. His father did not wait for him to come any closer, but he ran out of the house to meet his son. He put his arms around his neck and kissed him.

Then the son began to tell his father how sorry he was that he had been so bad. He asked his father if he could come back to live at his house.

His father was so glad to see him he would not let him say anything else. He called the servants to bring out new clothes to put on his son. And he put new shoes on his son's feet and a ring on his finger.

Then the father said, "Let's celebrate and be

happy, because my son has come back again. I thought he was lost, but now he is found."

Jesus told this story to teach that if we have done wrong, but now are sorry for it, all we need to do is go to our heavenly Father, God, and tell Him we are sorry.

1. What did the younger son in this story ask his father to give him?
2. After he had spent all his money, what did he have to do?
3. Will God forgive us if we come to Him and tell Him we are sorry for the things we did wrong and will not do them again?

You can find this story in your Bible in Luke 15:11-32.

55. Jesus Blesses Little Children

One day when Jesus was out teaching, some people brought little children to Him. They wanted Him to lay His hands on their heads and pray for them. But the disciples did not like this.

The disciples thought the children would bother Jesus. They knew that Jesus was busy teaching the people and they did not want anyone to interrupt Jesus while He taught. So they asked the people who brought the children to take them away.

In Jesus' time, some people did not think children were very important. They did not listen to what children had to say. They thought they should be quiet and stay out of the way of the grown-ups.

But Jesus was not like that. He was not pleased when the disciples said the people should take the children away. Jesus loved the children very much. He told the people to let the children come to Him and not to send them away. Then He took the children in His arms and sat them in His lap. He spoke kindly to them and prayed for them. He made them feel like they were just as important as everyone else.

And do you know what? Children are just as important as everyone else. God loves children just as much as grown-ups. And Jesus loves children. If they will love Jesus and obey what He says, Jesus will always remember the children and take care of them.

While Jesus was holding the children, He told the people around Him that the children were important. He also told them that we should all think of God the way children do. He meant that sometimes children know how to love God better than grown-ups do.

So Jesus loved the children and took time to hold them and pray for them. He did this another time when He was with the disciples. He asked

them to bring the children to Him so He could pray for them, so they would know they were important to Him and that He loved them.

Always remember that you are important to Jesus. He loves you very much and wants you to obey Him so you will have a happy life and act like God's child should.

1. While Jesus was teaching, who did some people bring to Jesus?
2. What did the disciples say when they saw the children?
3. What did Jesus tell the disciples when they wanted to send the children away?

You can find this story in your Bible in Matthew 19:13-15; Mark 10:13-16; and Luke 18:15-17.

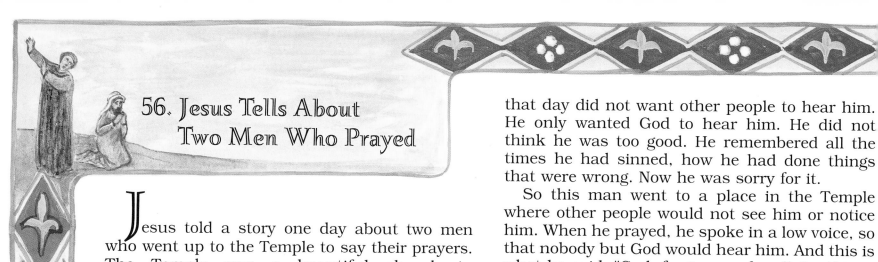

56. Jesus Tells About Two Men Who Prayed

Jesus told a story one day about two men who went up to the Temple to say their prayers. The Temple was a beautiful church in Jerusalem. People used to go to the Temple to say prayers to God.

One of these two men thought he was very good. He thought he was better than other people and he was proud. He wanted other people to think he was good, too. So he stood in a place in the Temple where other people could see him. Then he said his prayers in a loud voice. He wanted other people to see him and hear him pray. He thought they would say, "What a good man that must be who is saying his prayers over there."

The other man who went to the Temple to pray that day did not want other people to hear him. He only wanted God to hear him. He did not think he was too good. He remembered all the times he had sinned, how he had done things that were wrong. Now he was sorry for it.

So this man went to a place in the Temple where other people would not see him or notice him. When he prayed, he spoke in a low voice, so that nobody but God would hear him. And this is what he said: "God, forgive me for all the things I have done wrong."

After Jesus told the people this story, He talked to the people who were listening to Him. He said that God was more pleased with the second man than He was with the proud man.

Jesus said that God is not pleased with us when we are proud. When we are too proud, we want other people to look at us and think we are good. But God is pleased with us when we are sorry for the things we do wrong and when we ask God to forgive us. So Jesus said we should be like the man who prayed quietly instead of like the man who stood up and prayed loudly so others could hear him.

1. What did the two men in the story go to the Temple to do?
2. Did one of the men think he was very good?
3. What did the other man think of himself?
4. Where did the first man go to pray?
5. Where did the second man go to pray?
6. Which man did Jesus say God was most pleased with?

7. Is God pleased with us when we are too proud and when we want other people to praise us and call us good?
8. What does God want us to be sorry for?
9. Should we ask God to forgive us for our sins every day?

You can find this story in your Bible in Luke 18:9-14.

57. Jesus Says He Will Die on a Cross

Jesus had decided to go to the city of Jerusalem again. It was where the beautiful Temple was. As He walked to Jerusalem, He talked to His disciples. He told them that when they got to Jerusalem, there would be some people who did not love Jesus. They would be very mean to Him and would hurt Him. They would beat Him and spit on Him, and then they would kill Him.

Jesus had told the disciples this before. They were still not sure they understood what Jesus was talking about.

Jesus had come to earth as God's Son. God sent Jesus to tell all the people how much God loved them and that God wanted all people to be His children. But God knew that people did bad things, they sinned. And God wanted them to be sorry for the wrong things they did and stop doing them. So God sent Jesus to tell the people these things. Jesus also told people how to live their lives to please God.

But some people did not want to hear what Jesus had to say. They liked living their way. They liked doing things they wanted to do without caring if anyone else got hurt. They were selfish.

So when Jesus began to visit cities and talk about God, many people did not like it. They wanted to stop Jesus from teaching other people. After a while, they even wanted Jesus to go away and they thought the only way that would happen was if Jesus were killed. So some of these mean people began to try to figure out how they could kill Jesus.

Since Jesus was God's Son, He knew everything. He knew there were people who did not love Him. He knew there were people who wanted to kill Him, even though He loved them. And Jesus knew this would happen when they got to Jerusalem. So He tried to explain it to His disciples. He told His disciples that these cruel people would kill Him by nailing Him to a cross.

A cross was made of two large pieces of wood hooked together. In Jesus' time, sometimes people who did things that were very bad had to die by being nailed to a wooden cross. Jesus knew He would die the same way, even though He had not done anything wrong.

Jesus knew the people would lay Him down on the wooden cross and put big nails through His hands and His feet to attach Him to the cross so He could not get away. Then they would stick the cross in the ground and leave Jesus there until He died. Jesus told them that He would not stay dead, but would come alive again three days later.

The people would kill Jesus because they were angry with Jesus for telling them about the wrong they did, about their sins. They were also angry with Him for saying He was God's Son. These people were wicked and did not want to hear about their sins. They did not believe Jesus was God's Son.

1. Where were Jesus and His disciples going?
2. What did Jesus tell His disciples would happen to Him in Jerusalem?
3. How would the wicked people treat Jesus?
4. What would they nail Jesus to?
5. What is a cross made of?
6. What kind of people usually died on a cross?
7. Had Jesus done anything wrong?
8. Why did these wicked people want Jesus to die?
9. Did Jesus say He would stay dead or come alive again?

You can find this story in your Bible in Matthew 20:17-19; Mark 10:32-34; and Luke 18:31-34.

58. Jesus Heals Bartimaeus

On the way to Jerusalem, Jesus and His disciples came to a city called Jericho. There were a lot of people following Jesus and they crowded around Him as He walked along.

There was a blind man sitting in the street where they walked. His name was Bartimaeus. He sat in the street so he could beg for money from people who passed by. *Begging* was asking people to give him money so he could buy food to eat and clothes to wear. Bartimaeus had to beg because he was blind and could not work to have money for food and clothes.

When Bartimaeus heard the noise of the crowd, he asked the people what was happening. They told him that Jesus was passing by. Perhaps Bartimaeus had heard of Jesus because he called out in a loud voice, "Jesus, help me."

The people told him to be quiet. They did not want him to bother Jesus. But Bartimaeus only cried even louder, "Jesus, help me."

Then Jesus stopped walking and stood still. He told the people to bring Bartimaeus to Him. When Bartimaeus heard this, he was glad. He got up and hurried to Jesus, following the sound of His voice.

Then Jesus said to him, "What do you want me to do?"

Bartimaeus answered, "To make my eyes well, so that I might be able to see."

Then Jesus put out His hand and touched Bartimaeus' eyes. At once his eyes were well and he was able to see. Before that, Bartimaeus always had to let other people lead him, but now he walked down the street by himself. He followed after Jesus and spoke out loud, thanking God because he was made well.

1. Who was sitting in the street in Jericho as Jesus and His disciples came to the city?
2. When Bartimaeus heard the noise of the crowd, what did he do?
3. When Bartimaeus heard that Jesus was passing by, what did he cry out to Jesus?
4. Did the people tell him to be quiet?
5. What did Bartimaeus do then?
6. When Jesus asked Bartimaeus what he wanted Jesus to do, what did Bartimaeus say?
7. How did Jesus make his eyes well?
8. Did Bartimaeus thank God for sending Jesus to make him well?

You can find this story in your Bible in Mark 10:46-52 and Luke 18:35-43.

59. Jesus Meets Zacchaeus

In Jesus' country was a king. The king was the man who everyone in the country had to obey. The king said the people had to give him some of their money. This money was to pay for many things the king needed to run the country. It was called a tax.

So the king sent out men to take the money from the people. Some of these men were not good men. They took more money than the king asked for and kept some of it for themselves. So many people did not like these men who were called tax collectors.

One of these tax collectors was named Zacchaeus. Zacchaeus heard that Jesus was coming into the city and he wanted to see Jesus. As Jesus walked along the street, Zacchaeus could not see Jesus because the crowd was so big. Zacchaeus was a small man. He was not tall enough to see over the heads of the people in the crowd.

So Zacchaeus ran ahead of the crowd. There he climbed up in a tree so that he could see over the people. Then he waited for Jesus to come.

When Jesus came to the tree, He looked up and saw Zacchaeus. He told Zacchaeus to come down because He wanted to stay at his house that day. Then Zacchaeus climbed down and was very glad to take Jesus to his house.

Jesus told Zacchaeus many things, because Jesus knew about Zacchaeus. Zacchaeus promised to do all that Jesus told Him to do. He said he would be kind to poor people and give them some of his money to buy clothes and food.

Zacchaeus said if he had ever taken any money that did not belong to him, he would give it back to the people he took it from. Then Jesus told Zacchaeus that He would forgive him of all his sins so that God would not be angry with him.

If we want Jesus to forgive our sins, we must

be like Zacchaeus. We must be sorry for what we've done wrong and we must believe in Jesus. Then help people any way we can.

We must also be careful never to take anything that belongs to another person. If we have done that, we must give it back to them. This will please Jesus and He will forgive us as He forgave Zacchaeus.

1. When Zacchaeus could not see Jesus over the crowd, what did he do?
2. When Jesus came to the tree, what did He say to Zacchaeus?
3. Where did Zacchaeus take Jesus?

You can find this story in your Bible in Luke 19:1-10.

60. Jesus Sends for a Colt

As Jesus came near the city of Jerusalem, He told two of His disciples to go into a village, or little town, that was close by. He said they would find a donkey tied to a tree there and a little baby donkey, or colt, with it. Jesus told the disciples to untie them and bring them to Him.

Jesus also told them that if anyone asked why they were taking the donkey and the colt, they were to say that Jesus had sent for them. Then, Jesus said, the men would let the disciples take them.

So the disciples went to the nearby village and found the donkey and the colt tied there, just as Jesus had told them they would. As they untied them, some men asked why they were doing this. Then the disciples told them that Jesus had asked for them. So the men let the disciples take the donkey and the colt and they brought them to Jesus.

Jesus sat up on the colt and rode into the city of Jerusalem on the colt's back. A big crowd of people followed Him as He rode along. They all cried out, "Hosanna." They used this word to praise Jesus and thank Him for all He had done.

Some of the people took off their coats and laid them on the ground. Others cut down branches from the trees and laid them on the ground. They did this so Jesus could ride the colt over them.

They did all these things to show how glad they were to have Jesus come into their city. This was what the people would do whenever a king rode through their streets.

Then Jesus went up to the Temple that was in the city of Jerusalem. The people brought to Him others who were blind or lame, and Jesus made them well. That evening, Jesus went away from Jerusalem to a village called Bethany, which was not far away. He slept in Bethany that night.

1. What did Jesus send two of His disciples into a village to find?
2. What were they to do with the donkey and colt?
3. Where did Jesus ride the colt?
4. What did the people say when He rode into their city?
5. What did they put on the ground for Jesus to ride over?
6. Why did they do this?
7. Who did people bring to Jesus at the Temple?
8. Where did Jesus go to sleep that evening?

You can find this story in your Bible in Matthew 21:1-9; Mark 11:1-10; Luke 19:28-40; and John 12:12-19.

61. Jesus Tells a Story About a Vineyard

When Jesus went back to Jerusalem, He taught some of the people who gathered there. He taught them by telling them stories. One story He told was about a man who made a vineyard.

A vineyard is a place where grapes grow. Grapes grow on vines and the vines grow up around sticks in the ground. This man planted a lot of grapevines in the ground and made a vineyard.

Then he put up a fence around his vineyard. He also built a house in the vineyard and he sent some men to stay and take care of his grapevines while he went away. Then the man went on a trip to another country.

After a long time, when it was time for grapes to be ripe and ready to be picked off the vines, the man sent his servant to get some of his grapes for him. But the men who took care of his vineyard would not give the servant any grapes.

So the man sent another servant to get the grapes, but the men would not give him any grapes, either. In fact, the men threw stones at this servant and hurt him.

Then the owner of the vineyard said to himself, "What can I do to make these men do what I asked?"

Now the man had one son who he loved very much. He said, "This is what I will do. I will send my only son to them. They will be afraid to hurt my only son."

So the man's son went to the vineyard for his father. But when he got there, the men saw him coming. They said to each other, "Let us kill the man's son and take the vineyard for ourselves."

As soon as the man's son came into the vineyard, the men took him and killed him.

Jesus told this story to show what the wicked people in the city were going to do to Him. Jesus was God's only Son, like the son in the story. God had sent Him to tell the people they must love and obey Him. But instead of obeying God, the people who didn't love Jesus were going to kill God's Son, just like the wicked men in the vineyard.

1. What grows in a vineyard?
2. After the man in the story had planted his vineyard, where did he go?
3. Who did he tell to take care of his vineyard while he was gone?
4. Who did the man send to bring him some ripe grapes?
5. Would the men in the vineyard give the servant any grapes?
6. What did the men do to the second servant?
7. Finally, who did the man send back to the vineyard who he was sure they would obey?
8. What did the men in the vineyard do to the man's son?
9. Why did Jesus tell this story?
10. Whose Son was Jesus?
11. Had God sent Jesus to teach the people to love Him?
12. Instead of obeying God, what were the people going to do to Jesus?

You can find this story in your Bible in Matthew 21:33-46; Mark 12:1-12; and Luke 20:9-19.

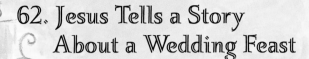

62. Jesus Tells a Story About a Wedding Feast

Then Jesus told the people another story. This was about a king who had a son who got married. The king held a wedding celebration with a big meal for many people, called a feast. When the feast was ready, the king sent his servants to tell the people that it was time for them to come. But they would not come.

So the king sent his servants again to tell them about all the good things waiting on the table for them to eat. But still the people did not come. Some of the people would not listen to the king's servants. Others of them listened, but would not obey. Some of the people were so wicked that they killed the king's servants.

When the king heard what they had done, he was very angry. He sent his soldiers to burn up the houses of the wicked people and to kill them.

Then the king called some other servants. He told them the feast was all ready but there was no one to eat the food.

So the king sent these servants to invite some other people to the feast. They were to go out into the streets and bring in everybody they met. So the servants brought back a lot of people to the feast.

These people did not have nice clothes to wear in the king's house. So the king had beautiful new clothes made for them. As soon as they had put on their new clothes, the king went into the room where the feast was ready, and sat down with the rest of the people.

But when the king came in, he saw a man there who was not wearing beautiful new clothes. He asked the man why he was not wearing the new clothes.

The man was ashamed and could not answer the king. He was too proud to take the new clothes, and thought his own clothes were good enough.

Then the king was angry and told his servants to take the man away from the feast and to punish him.

Jesus told this story to teach us that we must always want to obey God. God knows what is best for us and will not tell us to do anything that would be bad for us. But if we are not willing to do what God wants, God will not be pleased with us.

1. When the king sent his servants to tell the people to come to his feast, what did they do to his servants?
2. Where did the king send his servants afterward to find people to come to his feast?
3. When God asks us to obey Him, does He know what is best for us?

You can find this story in your Bible in Matthew 22:1-14 and Luke 14:15-24.

63. Jesus Tells Two Things We Must Do

Today, we have something that tells us the things God wants us to do. It is the Bible, God's book. In Jesus' time, people listened to Him to find out what God wanted them to do.

While Jesus was still in Jerusalem, a man came up to Him and asked Him what it was that God wanted us to do most. You see, many of the people then had a long list of rules they had made about how they thought God wanted them to live.

Long before Jesus came to earth, God had given the people a list of ten things He wanted them to do. They were rules for living their lives in a way that would please God and be best for them. We call these the Ten Commandments.

But the people kept adding rules to what God had given. Over the years, they had added so many rules to the list that it was hard to remember all of them. That is why the man asked Jesus His question. Of all the rules he'd heard of, he wanted to know which was the most important. What did God want people to do, most of all?

So Jesus told the man that the thing God wanted us to do most was to love Him.

We cannot see God, but He is so kind to us that we can love Him without seeing Him. Very often people who we love might go away where we cannot see them. But we keep on loving them even when we cannot see them.

We will see God one day, after we die, if we are His children. But God wants us to love Him now while we are still alive on earth. Then we can tell other people about God and how much He loves us. And we should love God more than we love anyone else. This is what Jesus told the man.

But then Jesus said there was a second thing that God wanted us to do that was also very important, besides loving Him. He wants us to love each other. If we love each other, we will be kind to each other. God is pleased with us when we are kind to each other.

So these are the two things Jesus said God wants us to do most--to love God and to love each other.

1. Whose book is the Bible?
2. What did the man ask Jesus?
3. What were the first things God told people He wanted them to do, many years before Jesus came to earth?
4. What did Jesus say God wants us to do more than anything else?
5. Is God pleased with us when we are kind to each other and love Him?

You can find this story in Matthew 22:34-40 and Mark 12:28-34.

64. The Pharisees Show Off

In Jesus' country there was a group of men called Pharisees. Many of the Pharisees lived in Jerusalem. They used to stand out in the streets to say their prayers. They did not pray in private or alone. They wanted people to hear them, because they wanted people to think they were good and to praise them.

The Pharisees were the men who tried to live by all the extra rules they had added to God's Ten Commandments. They did these things so they would look good to other people. They did not do them so God would be pleased. But God knew what they were really like because God could see them on the inside and knew what they were thinking.

The Pharisees were careful to do what was right only when people were looking at them. They only did this so people would think they were good. When nobody saw them, they did things that were wrong. God knew this, and so did Jesus.

Sometimes the Pharisees would try to trick Jesus. They would ask Him questions to see if He would give them a wrong answer. They were trying to find something Jesus did wrong so they could punish Him. But Jesus never did anything wrong. And He always answered their questions with just the right words.

But this only made the Pharisees angry with Jesus. They were really angry when Jesus told the people not to be like the Pharisees. He said that we must not say our prayers for other people to hear so that they will think we are good. When we pray we are talking to God. So God is the most important one to hear our prayers.

Jesus also said we must not do right only because we want others to think we are good. This was what the Pharisees did. We must do right because God tells us to do right, and because we want to please God.

When Jesus said these things, the Pharisees were even more angry with Him. Then they really wanted to find a way to get rid of Jesus. They wanted to keep living their lives the way they wanted. They did not want to listen to Jesus anymore.

1. Where did the men called Pharisees say their prayers?
2. Who did they really want to hear their prayers?
3. Why did they want people to hear them?
4. When anybody was looking at them, what were the Pharisees careful to do?
5. When nobody saw them, what did the Pharisees do?
6. Did Jesus say we should be like the Pharisees?
7. Who is it that we should want to hear us when we say our prayers?
8. Should we do right only when people are watching us?
9. Who sees us all the time?
10. Did the Pharisees get angry with Jesus?

You can find this story in your Bible in Matthew 23:1-36; Mark 12:38-40; and Luke 20:45-47.

65. A Poor Woman Gives Money

Remember that the Temple was a beautiful church in Jerusalem. Some priests lived at the Temple and the people who went there gave them money to take care of the Temple.

The people did not put this money into the priests's hands. Instead, they dropped their coins into a box that had a hole in the top. This box was on a table near the front door of the Temple.

Everyone who came in to the Temple dropped in as much money as he wanted. After a while, the ministers opened the box and took out the money that had been dropped in. With this money they bought things for the Temple. This money was the same as if it were given to God. It was God's money.

One day, Jesus saw the people who came into the Temple. He watched as they dropped their money into the box. Some people who were rich dropped in a lot of money all at once. After many people came through and dropped in a lot of money, Jesus noticed a woman who came into the Temple alone.

This woman was poor and she was a widow. Her husband had died so she had no one to work and make money for her. She did not have much money to give to the Temple. As Jesus watched the women, she dropped only a very small piece of money into the box.

Then Jesus called His disciples over to Him. He told them about the rich people dropping in lots of money and the poor widow dropping in only a small coin. Then He told the disciples that God was more pleased with the small piece of money that the poor woman gave than He was with the large pieces of money all the rich people gave.

The rich people had plenty of money. So even after they gave a lot of money to the Temple, they still had plenty of money left for themselves. But the poor woman had nothing left for herself. She gave all the money she had, even though it was only a little. She did not even have enough left over to buy bread to eat.

Jesus said that this showed how much the woman loved God. And God wants us to love Him more than He wants us to do anything else.

1. What did the people used to give to the priests who lived at the Temple?
2. What did they drop their money into?
3. Who did Jesus watch drop in a very small piece of money?

You can find this story in your Bible in Mark 12:41-44 and Luke 21:1-4.

66. Jesus Tells a Story About Young Women and Lamps

While He was still in Jerusalem, Jesus told another story about some young women who went out into the night, carrying oil lamps with them. In Jesus' time, people used lamps for light. These lamps were full of oil and had a piece of string going into the oil. They would light the string and the lamp would burn so they could see.

These young women went out at night with their lamps to meet a man who had just been married. This was a tradition in the days of Jesus. The man who got married would go home to his house and the young women would go out to meet him.

Each of these young women carried a lamp in her hand. But the man stayed longer than they expected. So the women sat down to wait for him and they all fell asleep.

In the middle of the night, someone woke the women and said, "The bridegroom is coming. Go out and meet him."

They all got up quickly and began to get ready. But they found that while they were asleep, their lamps had gone out. Without their lamps, the young women could not see where they were going.

Now some of the young women were wise. They had brought more oil with them, besides what was in their lamps. They poured this oil into their lamps and lighted them again. Then they were ready when the bridegroom came. And he took them into his house and invited them to a feast.

But the other young women were foolish. They did not bring any more oil with them. So they had to go buy some oil. By the time they got back, it was too late. The bridegroom had already gone into his house and shut the door.

Jesus told this story to teach us about Judgment Day. Jesus said He is coming back to earth again and that day will be called Judgment Day. Some people will be ready when He comes, and Jesus will take them up to heaven to be with God.

But some people will not be ready. These people will not go up to heaven with Jesus.

How can we be ready when Jesus comes back? We can love God, and be ready when He comes back to take us to heaven.

1. What did the young women who went out at night carry in their hands?
2. When the bridegroom stayed longer than expected, what did the young women do?
3. How can we be ready when Jesus comes back?

You can find this story in your Bible in Matthew 25:1-13.

67. Jesus Tells His Apostles About Judgment Day

Jesus talked with His disciples a lot about life on earth and how we should live with one another. But He also talked with them about heaven.

Jesus told His disciples about a day in the future. He called it Judgment Day. This day will be the time when Jesus comes back to take people to live with Him in heaven forever. Forever means there will be no more days and nights, or hours in the day. We will live in heaven with God and it will be different than life on earth. It will be better because we will not be hurt, or cry, or be sad. We will be happy to be with God and Jesus.

When Judgment Day comes, Jesus will come down from heaven and all the angels will come with Him. Then He will sit on a high seat, called a throne, like a king, where everyone can see Him.

All the people will be gathered together. You and I will see Jesus then. Everyone will see Him. The people who are dead and buried in their graves will come to life again on Judgment Day. Jesus will call to them, and they will hear Him and will come alive and stand where they can see Jesus.

Then the people who have loved Jesus and obeyed Jesus will stand on one side. The people who did wrong and did not ask God to forgive them and who did not obey Jesus will stand on the other side. Then Jesus will take all those who have loved Him up to heaven. But those who have not loved Jesus will be sent away from Him forever.

Jesus told His disciples that on Judgment Day, He will know what the people did for others, as well as whether or not they obeyed Him.

He said He would know if we gave food to people who were hungry or water to people who were thirsty. He would know if we invited people to stay with us when they needed a place to sleep or if we gave clothes to people who had no clothes. He said He would know if we visited people who were sick or lonely or in prison.

Then Jesus said if we did these things to help other people, it was as if we did these things for Jesus Himself.

But Jesus also said He would know if we did not do any of these things. It would be as if we did not do them for Jesus. And He has already taught us about loving each other. We show our love for each other by doing such things as giving people food, water, clothes, and a place to stay when they need them. We show our love by visiting people and taking care of them when they need help.

Jesus can see all these things when we do them. This shows we love each other, but it also shows we love Jesus because we are doing what He asked us to do. And this pleases God.

1. What did Jesus call the day He would come back to earth?
2. Who will come with Jesus?
3. What will it be like to live in heaven forever with Jesus?
4. Will you and I and everyone else see Jesus when He comes back on Judgment Day?
5. What will happen to the people who are dead and buried in graves?
6. How will Jesus separate the people on Judgment Day?
7. What will happen to the people who have not loved and obeyed Jesus?
8. Does Jesus know everything we do?

You can find this story in your Bible in Matthew 25:31-46.

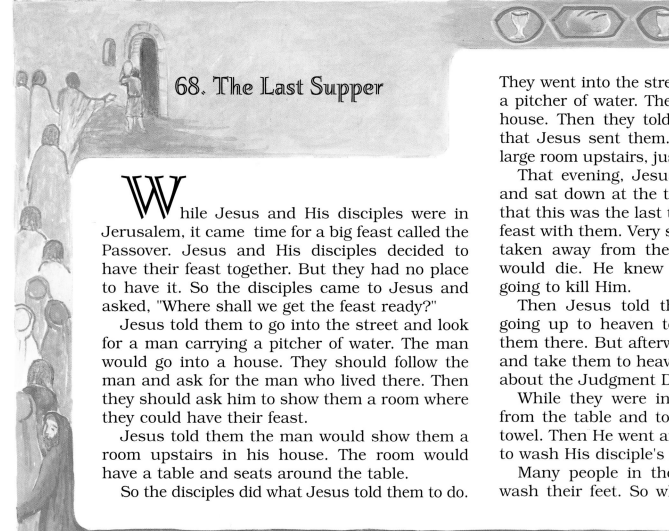

68. The Last Supper

While Jesus and His disciples were in Jerusalem, it came time for a big feast called the Passover. Jesus and His disciples decided to have their feast together. But they had no place to have it. So the disciples came to Jesus and asked, "Where shall we get the feast ready?"

Jesus told them to go into the street and look for a man carrying a pitcher of water. The man would go into a house. They should follow the man and ask for the man who lived there. Then they should ask him to show them a room where they could have their feast.

Jesus told them the man would show them a room upstairs in his house. The room would have a table and seats around the table.

So the disciples did what Jesus told them to do.

They went into the street and saw a man carrying a pitcher of water. They followed this man into a house. Then they told the man who lived there that Jesus sent them. The man showed them a large room upstairs, just like Jesus said he would.

That evening, Jesus came with the disciples and sat down at the table. He told His disciples that this was the last time He would ever eat the feast with them. Very soon, He said, He would be taken away from them. Jesus meant that He would die. He knew that wicked people were going to kill Him.

Then Jesus told the disciples that He was going up to heaven to make a place ready for them there. But afterward, He would come back and take them to heaven, too. Jesus was talking about the Judgment Day.

While they were in the room, Jesus got up from the table and took a bowl of water and a towel. Then He went around the table and began to wash His disciple's feet.

Many people in those days had servants to wash their feet. So when Jesus began to wash

His disciples' feet, the disciples were surprised. But Jesus did this to show His disciples how much He loved them.

Then the disciples and Jesus ate the meal. Jesus told them to remember Him whenever they ate the feast again. He wanted them to remember how much He loved them.

1. How did Jesus tell the disciples to find a place for their feast?
2. When Jesus met the disciples for the feast, what did He do with the water and towel?
3. Did He tell them to remember Him when they ate the feast again?

You can find this story in your Bible in Matthew 26:17-20; Mark 14:12-17; Luke 22:7-14; and John 13:1-20.

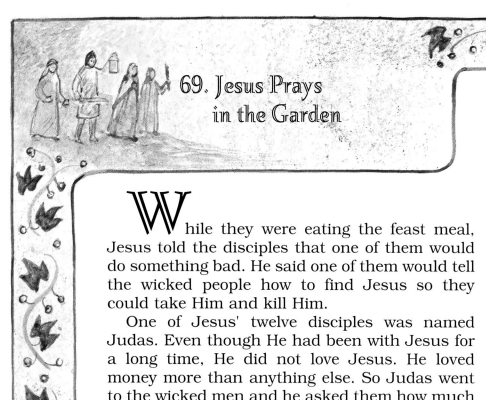

69. Jesus Prays in the Garden

While they were eating the feast meal, Jesus told the disciples that one of them would do something bad. He said one of them would tell the wicked people how to find Jesus so they could take Him and kill Him.

One of Jesus' twelve disciples was named Judas. Even though He had been with Jesus for a long time, He did not love Jesus. He loved money more than anything else. So Judas went to the wicked men and he asked them how much money they would give him to show them where Jesus was. The men told Judas they would give him thirty silver coins.

When Judas was sitting at the feast with Jesus, He heard Jesus say that He knew someone would tell the wicked men where to find Him.

Judas knew then that Jesus knew about what he had done. So Judas left the room to go find the wicked men.

Then Jesus and the rest of the disciples finished the meal and sang a song together. They left the house and walked to a place where there was a garden called Gethsemane.

It was night, and Jesus wanted to pray. So He asked most of His disciples to stay where they were but He took Peter and James and John with Him and asked them to wait in another place. Then Jesus went by Himself and kneeled down on the ground and prayed.

Jesus was very sad because He knew He was going to die. He also knew that if He died, it would show all the people how much God loved them, because Jesus was God's only Son. But He needed to pray to God to talk to His Father about how He felt. He told God that He would obey Him, but He asked Him to change things if He could.

Then He went back to check on His disciples. They were all asleep. He woke them up and asked them to stay awake so they could pray .

Then Jesus went back to pray again.

He prayed to God again and told God that He would obey Him. He went back to the disciples again. They had fallen back to sleep, because they were very tired. Jesus asked them again to pray to God and He went back to His place to pray again.

1. Which disciple did not love Jesus?
2. What did Judas ask the men who wanted to kill Jesus?
3. How much money did they promise to give Him?

You can find this story in your Bible in Matthew 26:14-16,21-25,36-46; Mark 14:10-11,18-20,32-42; Luke 22:3-6,39-46; and John 13:21-30.z

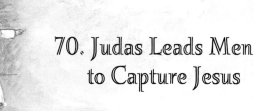

70. Judas Leads Men to Capture Jesus

Judas, the disciple who did not love Jesus, did not go to the garden with Jesus. But he knew where Jesus and His disciples would go after their supper. He had promised the wicked men he would show them where to find Jesus. He thought this night would be a good time to go tell the men who wanted to kill Jesus.

So Judas went to those men and told them where Jesus was. Then the men gave Judas the thirty silver coins they had promised him.

These wicked people sent some men with Judas to take Jesus. These men carried clubs and swords to fight with. They carried lanterns, too, so they could see in the dark. It was now the middle of the night. Judas went with the men to show them the way to the garden.

While the were going to the garden, Judas told the men how they would know which person was Jesus. Judas said as soon as they came into the garden, He would walk up to Jesus and kiss Him. Then the men would know that was Jesus and they could grab Jesus so He couldn't get away.

After Jesus finished praying in the garden, He went back to His disciples. Then they saw Judas coming into the garden with the wicked men. Judas walked up to Jesus and pretended he was glad to see Him. He even called Jesus "Master," which means teacher. Then Judas kissed Jesus.

As soon as He kissed Jesus, the wicked men took hold of Jesus and put ropes around Him so He could not get away.

1. Did Judas go with Jesus and the disciples into the garden after the feast?
2. When he saw where they had gone, who did he go to tell?
3. What did the wicked men give to Judas?
4. Did they send some more wicked men with Judas to take Jesus?
5. What did these men carry with them, to fight with?
6. How did Judas say they would know which man was Jesus?
7. After Judas kissed Jesus, what did the wicked men do to Jesus?

You can find this story in your Bible in Matthew 26:47-56; Mark 14:43-52; Luke 22:47-53; and John 18:2-12.

71. Peter Denies Jesus

When the disciples saw the men put ropes around Jesus, they were angry. They wanted to fight the other men. The disciple named Peter took a sword and hit one of the men with it. He cut off the man's ear. But Jesus told Peter to put away his sword. Then Jesus touched the man's ear and made it well again.

Jesus did not want the disciples to fight for Him. He said that God would send angels from heaven to fight for Him if He asked. But Jesus would not ask for them. He was willing to let the men take Him, even though He knew they would kill Him.

Jesus was willing to let the men kill Him because that was how He was going to be punished in our place for all the sins we had done.

This way, God would show all people how much He loved them and how He would forgive them for their sins. Then people would not be punished for their sins if they told God they were sorry for what they'd done wrong.

The men took Jesus out of the garden. The disciples were afraid the men might take them too, so they all ran away.

Jesus had told Peter that there would come a time when people would ask him if he knew Jesus. He said that Peter would tell them he did not know Jesus. He said Peter would do this three times before the rooster crowed in the early morning. But Peter had told Jesus he would never do that. He would always tell people he knew Jesus and loved Jesus.

When the disciples ran off, Peter went to sit where he could watch where they had taken Jesus. He sat far enough away so no one would see him. But a woman came to him and asked him if he was one of the men with Jesus. Peter told the woman he was not with Jesus.

Later someone else asked him if he was with

Jesus, but Peter said he was not. Then one more time someone asked him again and he said no for the third time. At that moment Peter heard the rooster crow and he remembered what Jesus had said to him. And he was very sad.

1. Did the disciples want to fight the wicked men when they saw them put ropes around Jesus?
2. What did Peter do?
3. Did Jesus want them to fight?
4. What did Jesus do to the man's ear?
5. Why did Jesus not call angels from heaven to help him?
6. Why was Jesus willing to die?
7. When the men took Jesus from the garden, what did the disciples do?
8. What had Jesus told Peter he would say about Jesus?
9. Did Peter tell people he did not know Jesus?
10. How many times did he do this?
11. How did Peter feel when he heard the rooster crow?

You can find this story in your Bible in Matthew 26:51-58,69-75; Mark 14:47-50,66-72; Luke 22:49-51,54-62; and John 18:10-11,16-18,25-27.

72. Jesus Dies on the Cross

In that country there was a man called the governor. He was the one who punished people who did wrong. The men who wanted to kill Jesus brought Him to the governor. They told the governor that Jesus had done wrong and that He should be punished.

These men wanted to get rid of Jesus because they did not want to hear Him talk about their sins. They wanted Jesus to go away.

They told the governor that Jesus was wicked and ought to be killed. Then the governor was very cruel to Jesus. He beat Him with a whip.

A crowd soon gathered to see what was happening to Jesus. The crowd began to yell and many of the people wanted Jesus to die.

The soldiers were also cruel to Jesus. They beat Him and spit on Him. They knocked Him down on the ground and made fun of Him. Then the governor told some soldiers to take Jesus away and kill Him.

The soldiers got a cross made of wood. They made Jesus carry the heavy cross down the road to the place where He would die. When they got to a hill outside the city, the soldiers laid Jesus down on the cross with His arms stretched out. Then they put big nails through His hands and His feet and nailed Him to the cross.

They made a hole in the ground and dropped the end of the cross into the hole. The soldiers stayed there and watched Him die. They did not believe Jesus was God's Son.

Some of the people who loved Jesus were also there. They cried because they were so sad that Jesus had been killed.

One of the people was a rich man named Joseph. When Joseph saw that Jesus was dead, he asked the governor to let him take Jesus down from the cross and bury Him. The governor said he could do this.

Joseph wrapped up Jesus' dead body in some new, clean pieces of cloth. A man named Nicodemus helped Joseph. The two men buried Jesus in a cave that was dug out of a large rock. Then the men rolled a big stone in front of the opening to the cave.

Then the governor sent some soldiers to watch the cave. They wanted to keep Jesus' disciples away from where Jesus was buried.

1. Was the governor cruel to Jesus?
2. What did the crowd do to Jesus?
3. What did the soldiers nail Jesus to?

You can find this story in your Bible in Matthew 27:1-66; Mark 15:1-47; Luke 23:1-56; and John 18:28-19:42.

73. Jesus Comes Alive Again

In the night, while it was dark and quiet, God sent an angel down from heaven. The angel's face was bright, like lightning. His clothes were white as snow. When the soldiers saw the angel, they were afraid. They shook and fell on the ground. They could not move. The angel came to the cave and rolled the stone away from the door. This was a heavy stone, too heavy for a man to move alone. But the angel rolled it away.

And then a miracle happened. Jesus was not in the tomb! He was alive and He was not there!

You remember how Jesus had told His disciples long before this that the people who did not love Him would kill Him. But He also told His disciples that He would come to life again. They did not understand what He meant. But now Jesus had done what He said. He had come alive and gone out of the grave after the people buried Him.

The women who had gone to see where Jesus was buried came back to the grave early Sunday morning. They wanted to make sure Jesus' body was prepared for the grave. In those days, people put spices and ointments on a body before it was buried. They did not have time to do this before, so they were going to the grave to do it now.

When the women got to the grave, they noticed something different. The stone was no longer in front of the cave door. And when they looked inside the cave, Jesus' body was not there. Then they saw an angel in bright white clothing. They were afraid, but the angel told them not to be afraid. The angel said that Jesus had come back to life. Jesus was alive again!

The women were so happy. They hurried to find the disciples to tell them the wonderful news that Jesus was alive again.

1. Who did God send down to Jesus' grave in the night?
2. How did the soldiers feel when they saw the angel?
3. What did the angel do to the stone in front of the cave door?
4. Who went to the grave early Sunday morning?
5. What did they go to the grave to do?
6. What did the women see when they got to the grave?
7. Where did the women go when they left the grave?

You can find this story in your Bible in Matthew 28:1-8; Mark 16:1-8; Luke 24:1-12; and John 20:1-13.

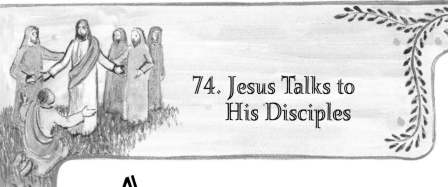

74. Jesus Talks to His Disciples

After Jesus came out of the grave, Jesus went to see His disciples. They were all in a room together and the door of the room was locked shut. Suddenly, Jesus was in the room with them.

When the disciples saw Jesus standing there, they were afraid. They thought it could not be Jesus. They thought He was dead.

But Jesus told them not to be afraid. Then He showed them His hands and His feet with the marks of the nails in them. He did this so they would know that it was Jesus and that He was really alive again.

Then Jesus ate with them to prove that He was really alive.

Jesus also appeared to the women who had come to His grave. Many other times He went to the disciples in different places. He did this because He wanted them to be sure that He was really alive. They needed to know so they could tell other people about this miracle, that Jesus had died and now was alive again.

While He was with His disciples, Jesus told them many things. He told them they must go and tell all the people how He had died. He told them to tell people that when Jesus died on the cross, He was punished in the place of all other people so they would never have to die for the wrong things they had done, for their sins.

Jesus told the disciples to tell the people in their country about what He had done. But He also told them to go to people in other countries and all over the world so that everyone would hear about Jesus. Jesus wanted everyone to know that He was God's Son and that God loves them so much that He sent Jesus to die so that the people would not be punished for their sins. Jesus also wanted everyone to know that they could be God's children if they were sorry for their sins and believed that He had come alive again.

Jesus wanted you and me to know about this, too. He wanted us to know how much He loved us so we would love Him. He wanted us to be willing to do what He tells us to do. If we love and believe in Jesus, God will forgive us and take us to be His children.

1. After Jesus came out of the grave, who did He go talk with?
2. Were the disciples together in a room?
3. Was the door closed?
4. Who appeared suddenly in the room?
5. Why were the disciples afraid?
6. What did Jesus show the disciples so they would know He was really alive again?
7. Who else did Jesus go to see?
8. Did Jesus see the disciples in other places after He was alive again?
9. What did Jesus tell His disciples to tell others about Him?
10. Did Jesus only want them to tell people in their own country?
11. Does Jesus want you and me to know about how He died on the cross for all people?
12. Why does Jesus want us to know about Him?

You can find this story in your Bible in Luke 24:36-43 and John 20:19-23.

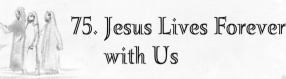

75. Jesus Lives Forever with Us

After Jesus had talked with His disciples, He took them out of the city to a place by themselves. He spoke to them and reminded them of all the things He had taught them while He had been with them. He told them again that they must begin to tell people about Him in their country and throughout the whole world. And He told them that He would always be with them and would help them remember the things He taught them.

While Jesus was speaking with the disciples, all at once He began to go up from them toward the sky. He went up higher and higher, until they saw Him go into a cloud. Then they could not see Him anymore.

After that, two angels came and spoke to the disciples. They told the disciples that Jesus had gone up to heaven. Then the disciples went back to the city and thanked God for all they had seen.

Jesus is in heaven now, but He looks down from there and sees all the little children who love Him and believe in Him. He hears them when they pray to Him, and He helps them to be good.

You must never be afraid, because Jesus will never forget you. He loves you and will always take care of you. When He comes back to earth one day, He will call all His children to Him and take them up to heaven. Then they will live with Him there always.

1. After Jesus had talked with His disciples, where did He take them?
2. While He was speaking to them, where did He begin to go?
3. What did Jesus go up into?
4. After that, could they see Jesus anymore?
5. Who came then and spoke to the disciples?
6. Where did the angels say Jesus had gone?
7. Where is Jesus now?
8. Does Jesus see all the children who love Him and believe in Him?
9. Does Jesus ever forget you?
10. Does He love you and take care of you?
11. Where will He take you when He comes back to earth?
12. How long will we stay with Jesus in heaven?

You can find this story in your Bible in Mark 16:19; Luke 24:44-53; and Acts 1:4-11.